Literacy Moments

Literacy Moments

Creating Daily Teachable Moments with Beginning Readers

Jacqueline Witter-Easley

ROWMAN & LITTLEFIELD
Lanham • Boulder • New York • London

Published by Rowman & Littlefield
An imprint of The Rowman & Littlefield Publishing Group, Inc.
4501 Forbes Boulevard, Suite 200, Lanham, Maryland 20706
www.rowman.com

6 Tinworth Street, London SE11 5AL, United Kingdom

Copyright © 2019 by Jacqueline Witter-Easley

All rights reserved. No part of this book may be reproduced in any form or by any electronic or mechanical means, including information storage and retrieval systems, without written permission from the publisher, except by a reviewer who may quote passages in a review.

British Library Cataloguing in Publication Information Available

Library of Congress Cataloging-in-Publication Data

Names: Witter-Easley, Jacqueline, author.
Title: Literacy moments : creating daily teachable moments with beginning / Jacqueline Witter-Easley.
Description: Lanham : Rowman & Littlefield, [2019] | Includes bibliographical references.
Identifiers: LCCN 2019005139 (print) | LCCN 2019013368 (ebook) | ISBN 9781475847345 (electronic) | ISBN 9781475847321 (cloth : alk. paper) | ISBN 9781475847338 (pbk. : alk. paper)
Subjects: LCSH: Reading (Elementary) | Reading (Elementary)—Activity programs.
Classification: LCC LB1573 (ebook) | LCC LB1573 .W588 2019 (print) | DDC 372.4—dc23
LC record available at https://lccn.loc.gov/2019005139

Contents

Foreword ... vii
Catherine Compton-Lilly

Introduction ... ix

Part 1: Creating a "Literacy Moments" Learning Environment—An Introduction ... 1

1 Do You Have What It Takes? Nurturing Joyful Readers ... 3

2 Cultivating a Vibrant Classroom Library with Culturally Responsive Books ... 11

3 Empowering Beginning Readers through Author Studies ... 25

Part 2: Literacy Moments for Word Recognition and Vocabulary Development—An Introduction ... 35

4 Immersing Students in a Print-Rich "Literacy Moments" Environment ... 39

5 Integrating Popular Culture to Facilitate Foundational Literacy Skills ... 51

6 Integrating the Arts into Literacy Instruction ... 65

Part 3: Literacy Moments for Developing Comprehension Processes—An Introduction ... 85

7 Pre-Reading Literacy Moments That Foster Comprehension ... 87

8	Literacy Moments That Foster Comprehension during Reading	95
9	Post-Reading Activities	107

Appendix: Diverse Children's Authors and Their Birthdays 117
Reference List 121
Children's Books Cited 125
About the Author 129

Foreword

"Wow, are you ever lucky that you picked up this book!" This is what I imagine saying to prospective readers as they open this book. You have found a book that is truly useful to literacy educators. Your luck is not happenstance. It is intentional and only possible because it was written by an experienced teacher and teacher educator. The book's author, Jacqueline Witter-Easley, has crafted a book that resides at the intersection of long-term experience and careful thought. It offers voice, expertise, and relevance to educators who want to create and capitalize on teachable literacy moments that can add up to literate lives.

Dr. Witter-Easley describes the need to help emerging readers attend to both visual and non-visual information. You will find the same types of information in this book. Helpful visual information includes tables, illustrations, and bulleted lists of children's books, songs, and instructional activities. Non-visuals are even more important. They are the book's content, the information and ideas presented, the lovely writing style, and Witter-Easley's understandings of what you—as the reader—already know and want to learn next.

Her lessons and suggestions are grounded in years of teaching and in years of working with preservice teachers who are just starting to explore the intricacies of masterful teaching. While Witter-Easley insists on using authentic texts with children, as a teacher, you insist on authentic professional texts that address real classrooms, full of active children, and lived challenges. You demand books that introduce real readers and invite you into living and breathing schools and classrooms.

In Chapter 4, Witter-Easley writes, "Beginning readers are busy people." As she explains, children work hard as they learn to decode words, solve math problems, complete assignments, and make friends. They exert energy as they play and interact with friends and family. Because of this, learning to read must be engaging and intentional. Witter-Easley has designed a book that helps teachers to make teaching intentional and productive. In this book, reading processes are developed, classroom contexts are staged, and literacy moments are created. This requires thoughtful, resourceful, and committed teachers, and the ideas in this book are sure to inspire and assist teachers as they create and sustain intentional classrooms that support children.

Just as emergent readers assemble interactive reading systems entailing skills, meaning, and multiple sources of information, teachers assemble interactive and nuanced teaching systems that include instructional strategies, attention to learning contexts, individual children, and awareness of cultural and linguistic differences. The list is endless, and everything on it happens simultaneously and continuously. Luckily, Witter-Easley understands this complexity and makes information accessible.

The book invites teachers on a journey starting with their own reading habits and curiosities; she then considers classroom spaces and classroom libraries. She describes reading road trips, teacher book clubs, and becoming book browsers. Readers then explore powerful literacy moments that present opportunities for children to experiment with reading strategies, explore new words, and engage with text in print-rich classrooms. These classrooms feature both traditional and contemporary texts across a range of modalities.

For Witter-Easley, authentic and personally significant texts invite readers to a pinnacle where processing culminates and results in understanding and thoughtful readings of texts. The child is always at the center of Witter-Easley's reading process, and understanding text is both the goal and the incentive for becoming a reader.

So, count your blessings, and dig in.

Catherine Compton-Lilly, EdD
John C. Hungerpiller Professor of Education
University of South Carolina

Introduction

"Wow, you're lucky. Your first graders love to read." This comment came to me from the school librarian one morning after my students finished checking out books during their weekly library visit. The children had enthusiastically shared with the librarian their excitement about finding a book either by a favorite author, or about a favorite subject, or any number of reasons. Library time was a favorite among them, and this love of reading increased as the school year progressed.

Many years later, in my role as a teacher educator and professor of reading methods courses, I reflected on this statement with satisfaction. Each semester I promote to my elementary education majors the importance of facilitating their future students' love of reading. I have come to realize in my reflective thinking about this comment, however, that the librarian's use of the word "luck" is significant. To me, "luck" is not happenstance; rather, it is the resulting effect caused when preparation and opportunity meet.

So, when the opportunity to check out library books arose for my students, how had I prepared them to seize this moment with enthusiasm and success? My answer: I prepared them every day by creating opportunities through daily activities in which I engaged my beginning readers in real-world reading and writing occasions, weaving the necessary skills into the fabric of their encounters with authentic text. In other words, I created a classroom rich with literacy moments.

My integration of reading skills into authentic text developed early in my teaching career and is based on Rumelhart's (1994) Interactive Theory of reading. This theory postulates that beginning readers approach a text using both visual and non-visual information. The visual information includes the features and shapes of letters, the letter names, the letter clusters, and the blending of the letter sounds within a cluster to create a word. The non-visual information includes the syntax (grammatical structures of a sentence), the semantics (contextual information conveyed in a sentence or paragraph), and the reader's schema (background knowledge about the content and about how language works).

All of the sources of visual and non-visual information interact simultaneously in a reader's mind, allowing her to predict and read each word in a given text. In other words, the act of reading is not linear, relying first on the visual information and finally on the non-visual information. Instead, the act of reading involves the ability to concurrently use visual and non-visual information to construct a text's meaning.

Teaching beginning readers how to identify and sound out letters to read words will empower children to read successfully. However, without positioning such lessons within the context of authentic texts, fledgling readers may increase their word recognition skills but will lack the ability to use non-visual information to facilitate their reading skills. Furthermore, without the use of meaningful text to teach reading skills, beginning readers' desire to read for pleasure and for lifelong learning will likely diminish over the years.

Therefore, teachers of beginning readers must create learning environments that embrace the interactive theory: teaching both the skill of reading words along with the ability to comprehend text and use non-visual information simultaneously. In other words, teachers who develop literacy moments throughout their day will attend to both the visual and non-visual information, thereby increasing both their students' ability to read words and to mature into lifelong readers.

In this book, readers will find a variety of research-based teaching methods that will enable them to create literacy moments for the beginning readers in their classrooms. Each chapter provides information about how to use a variety of authentic texts (picture books, articles, song lyrics, poems, recipes, etc.) to facilitate the intentional teaching of specific foundational skills—both visual (word recognition, vocabulary) and non-visual (syntactical and semantic information to enhance comprehension processes).

The book is organized into three sections that will guide early elementary teachers in their professional development of creating opportunities for teachable moments that will enhance their students' literacy skills. The first section will focus on establishing a "Literacy Moments" learning environment. This section will include chapters that convey information about developing teachers' personal reading habits, developing a vibrant classroom library that contains culturally responsive texts, and promoting a love of reading through author studies.

The next section will target specific literacy moments that address foundational skills (word recognition skills, vocabulary), such as: creating a print-rich environment, integrating popular culture (i.e., song lyrics, rhymes/chants, current events), and integrating the arts.

The final section will focus on comprehension and critical thinking skills, with chapters specifically dedicated to each phase of reading a text: pre-reading activities, during reading activities, and post-reading activities. These chapters will provide methods and activities that use meaningful contexts of literature, poetry, informational texts, etc., to facilitate comprehension skills throughout the reading process.

The goal of this book is to immerse teachers in the concept of literacy moments so that they will experience a mindset shift in which they begin to create their own literacy moments with their students. This book is intended to give teachers the tools to nurture joyful readers by infusing their classrooms' daily lives with authentic literacy moments every day.

REFERENCES

Rumelhart, D. E. (1994). Toward an interactive model of reading. In R. B. Ruddell, M. R. Ruddell, & H. Singer (Eds.), *Theoretical models and processes of reading* (4th ed.) (pp. 864–94). Newark, DE: International Reading Association.

Part 1

Creating a "Literacy Moments" Learning Environment— An Introduction

Before we delve into the specifics of infusing literacy moments into the early-elementary classroom, it is important to set the stage. In other words, if we truly want to effectively incorporate moments of literacy development across our curriculum, then we must first establish a learning environment that embodies literacy as a way of life. In the first three chapters, readers will find information that serves this purpose. The chapters serve to encourage teachers to reflect on the learning environments they create, in both affective and physical domains of literacy development.

Chapter 1 engages teachers in reflecting on their own reading habits. The premise here is to encourage us all to think about ourselves as readers and how our own reading habits (or lack thereof) influence our abilities to foster our beginning readers' love of reading. Upon our self-assessment of our reading habits, we may find that we need to increase our recreational reading activity by intentionally seeking creative ways to fit this into our lives. In doing so, we will not only enhance the quality of our own lives, we will enhance our ability to model to our students a love of reading. In other words, we will truly be able to walk the talk with our students.

When teachers intentionally model their own reading habits as ways of enriching the quality of life, they establish a positive affective domain in their classrooms. Their rooms are communities of readers and writers who motivate one another daily in their quest for developing their literacy lives. For those teachers who do not see themselves as readers, or perhaps do not see themselves as consistently attending to the care and feeding of their literacy lives, I provide a variety of methods and techniques for increasing and cultivating your literacy habits. The key is to be intentional in seeking opportunities for engaging with literature.

Another key to establishing a classroom conducive to providing authentic literacy moments that motivate beginning readers to develop their own reading habits is through the effective use and selection of books in the classroom library. Chapter 2 guides teachers in the selection of books written by and about diverse members of our society. In this way, books act as both mirrors that reflect our cultural diversity as well as windows that allow us to see the world beyond our own diverse experiences. When teachers set aside time to critically review their libraries' collections, they ensure that more voices are heard and that their students will engage with texts that validate and enhance their personal identities.

While setting up a culturally responsive collection of books in the classroom library provides a significant enhancement to the affective domain of the classroom, as well as addresses the physical domain of creating space for literature, we need to take this further. We must also intentionally create literacy moments that infuse these books into the curriculum so that students have opportunities to interact with them on a daily basis. Therefore, Chapter 2 includes specific strategies for enticing students to read the books through interactive book displays. These displays promote literacy by increasing students' awareness of various genres, authors, and subjects found on the shelves of their library. Teachers must set aside time for students to read these books. This chapter also includes methods for facilitating silent reading time as well as consistent moments enhanced through teachers reading aloud to their students.

Once teachers enhance their personal reading habits, infuse their classroom libraries with culturally responsive books, and intentionally seek ways to increase their students' access to these books through displays and time for reading, they are ready to focus their overall environment on developing their students' self-efficacy in reading by integrating author studies into the classroom. Chapter 3 provides the framework for creating author studies by addressing their affective benefits in empowering beginning readers' abilities to select books independently, see themselves as consumers of literature, and develop their critical thinking skills through discussions that compare and contrast books and authors. The chapter also includes specific activities that promote these benefits, as well as basic reading skills. Additionally, teachers will find selection criteria for determining which authors to study, as well as suggestions for developing an Author-of-the-Month program.

It is my goal to have Part 1 set the foundation for establishing an early-elementary classroom that is ready to capitalize on literacy moments throughout their daily routines. When teachers are readers and intentionally create a learning environment that addresses the intangible elements of intrinsic motivation to read, they will have the mindset in place to fully embrace teachable moments as opportunities to expand their students' literacy development.

Chapter One

Do You Have What It Takes?
Nurturing Joyful Readers

Elementary teachers work hard to create a learning environment that is colorful, engaging, and rich in print. These are all important elements in creating a physical domain that promotes literacy. However, the intangible, affective domain must also be attended to by classroom teachers. The affective domain refers to the learning climate in a classroom. How can teachers positively impact their students' motivation and desire to learn and to read? According to Applegate & Applegate (2004), "intrinsically motivated readers engage in reading for its own sake and enjoy satisfying their own curiosity" (p. 554).

An important component of creating a climate that nurtures positive attitudes toward reading is for the classroom teacher to be a reader her/himself. Teachers who read for recreation and to satisfy curiosity are well positioned to authentically share with their students their own literacy experiences. They speak from personal experience and model the reading life for their students. Put simply, they walk the talk. It stands to reason to expect that teachers who read for pleasure will be more influential and effective in motivating their students to become lifelong readers (Ruddell, 2005).

Applegate & Applegate (2004) referred to this as the Peter Principle, based on the biblical passage from Acts 3:5, in which the Apostle Peter responded to a crippled man's request for money "that he could not give what he did not have" (p. 556). Therefore, the first step in developing an affective classroom environment that motivates students to read is for teachers to reflect on their personal reading habits. They should ask themselves: *Do I have what it takes to motivate beginning readers to develop their own reading habits? Do I, myself, have a "reading habit"?*

Teachers who find themselves reflecting on a lack of personal time spent reading will be well served, as will their students, to cultivate a personal reading habit. Following are some effective, easy-to-implement ideas for increasing the reading habit so that teachers can authentically give their students the gift of motivation to read on their own.

READING ROAD TRIPS

Audiobooks are recorded oral readings of published books—in all genres. Teachers with a longer commute to work, or who take a road trip over summer break, will find that simply planning ahead and obtaining an audiobook from their local public library will increase their own exposure to a variety of books without the stress of trying to fit time into their busy days to sit and read. Most public libraries provide access to apps for smart phones that contain a variety of ebooks and audiobooks available for check out.

Library patrons simply download the app, input their library card number, and they have access to the library's collection at their fingertips! Popular apps owned by public libraries include: Overdrive™, Hoopla™, and Libby™. When the books are downloaded to the phone, they are checked out to that patron for a specified loan time (typically two to three weeks). Once the loan period has ended, the book is removed from the device. This is a very accessible, thrifty method to increase teachers' reading habits. It is also a very enjoyable way to navigate traffic and escape a stressful work day!

TEACHER BOOK CLUB

When teachers develop their own community of readers, they model to their students the power of books to connect with others. Teachers can nurture their own reading habits by establishing a Teacher Book Club. While reading professional books would be one approach, it would be more effective for teachers to read books from all genres, for both adults and children. Teachers could meet once each month during their lunch break to discuss their chosen books.

This basic idea has significant ramifications with beginning readers because teachers can make their own reading habits visible to their students by including them in their reading process. By keeping their current book-club book on their desk, students will see that their teachers are readers. During silent reading time, teachers could take their book from their desk and read it. Silent reading time must be spent reading—by both the students and the teacher! This provides an authentic model of "walking the talk" for the students.

Furthermore, by taking time to discuss the book as it is being read, including personal insights and reactions, the students will witness the thought processes of a successful reader. Finally, teachers should tell the students when the Teacher Book Club will meet and share with the students some of the insights the other teachers noted during the discussion. This powerful practice serves two purposes: it increases the teacher's reading habit, and it provides authentic modeling of participation in the "literacy club" (Smith, 1988, p. 2).

BE A BOOK BROWSER

Teachers can schedule time after school, at least once a month, to make a date with themselves and go to their public library to browse the latest book displays, read the library newsletters, and chat with the librarian on the latest best sellers. This is a wonderful way to browse books, get to know current authors, and develop a network of literacy professionals to guide readers through the library collection.

Over the last decade, libraries have shifted into centers of technology, and many have moved their catalogs online. This is very convenient, but it also has an unintended consequence: fewer patrons are entering the library building and immersing themselves in the vast possibilities of the collection. By making time to intentionally browse the physical space of the library, teachers will become acquainted with the wide array of books available, will likely develop new interests in informational topics on display, and will increase their knowledge base on new authors and genres based on librarians' recommendations. This will likely empower teachers who haven't been active readers because they will have knowledge about authors and develop their own personal favorites to follow and read their latest publications.

AVOID THE SUMMER SLUMP

Students aren't the only ones who suffer from the summer slump—adults do, too, if they don't take advantage of this time to catch up on their reading! Teachers can increase their own reading habits by simply challenging themselves to read four books by the summer's end. Since there are generally three months set aside for summer holiday, challenging oneself to read four books means reading a little more than a book a month.

This is very effective for non-readers because it is a short-term challenge and it is very manageable, given the gift of time most teachers have because they are not busy with lesson preparations, bulletin board creation, and learning center development! They're not grading papers, gathering supplies, or participating in committee work. This, of course, doesn't mean that teachers are not busy during the summer—most continue to research new content for disciplinary units of study, develop materials and manipulatives for use during the school year, create lesson plans related to new themes, books, etc., or even take continuing education courses.

However, with the slowed-down nature of this season comes opportunity to nurture the reading habit by taking a daily break from classroom preparations and sitting outside reading a good book. If teachers don't intentionally prioritize their time for reading, it can easily fall by the wayside. Therefore, they can create a reading challenge to avoid the summer slump—and tell the students about the books read over the summer when they return to school in the fall.

FOLLOW BOOK-RELATED PAGES IN SOCIAL MEDIA

Many teachers have favorite social media pages that they follow for teaching advice. The next step is for teachers to take this opportunity to think of social media as a way to enhance their book knowledge so that they'll be empowered to select new books at their libraries for personal reading pleasure. Several social media pages are focused solely on developing adults as readers. Here are a few:

- EveryLibrary™—This page posts information and articles related to developing reading habits among adults. It also encourages wide usage of public libraries.

- Book Riot™—This page posts informal articles about books around a topic, author, or series. It engages the reader in exploring new genres or topics and provides excellent must-read recommendations! To take reading further, Bookriot.com publishes an annual "Read Harder" challenge in which it lists twenty-four categories of books to encourage readers to intentionally select diverse books for their reading pleasure each year.

- Goodreads™—This is a network-generating site and app that creates an online literacy community. Subscribers to this site log books they've read, set an annual personal reading challenge, review and recommend books, and list books they'd like to read. Subscribers network with friends to get updates on books they've read or want to read. The app generates personal recommendations based on recently completed books. Finally, by following this site on social media, readers receive posts containing information on new authors, books, and events.

- Read It Forward™—This site posts recommendations for book clubs' reading selections, as well as creative sets of books around themes and topics. Their positive messages inspire adults to participate in a literate community.

BOOK CHATS

Either in person or online, carving out time once a week to chat with colleagues about good books is an effective way to discuss new authors, recommend great reads, and basically encourage one another to spend time reading. Just like people who exercise with friends, people who read with friends are likely to maintain their reading habits. Set aside lunch time once a week to commit to bringing along a couple of books. Talk about them, recommend them, and, ultimately, loan them to one another. This is a powerful moment for students to witness while they eat lunch in the cafeteria, too!

READING LOGS

Many teachers of beginning readers use reading logs to encourage their students to develop a reading habit. They require their students to keep track of books they read and may even expect parents to sign the log each evening to verify that the students completed their reading time. What if the teacher also maintained a reading log and kept it on the desk so the students could see that their teacher participates in this form of literacy development? This is another powerful opportunity to demonstrate a personal reading habit while also nurturing the teacher's ability to increase time spent reading for pleasure.

AWARD-WINNING READING SELECTIONS

A natural source for selecting quality children's literature is on the American Library Association's website (www.ala.org). Teachers of beginning readers should refer to this resource to locate well-written children's books of all genres, by culturally diverse authors, and for a variety of age levels. The Newbery Award is given to a book written and published in the United States in a given year. These books tend to be written for upper-elementary and middle school grade levels. They are excellent for reading aloud to beginning readers, however, and therefore make for worthwhile books to read for pleasure. Teachers will develop their reading habits and increase their repertoire of classroom read-aloud books.

For books by diverse authors, teachers should become acquainted with the following American Library Association awards: Coretta Scott King Award (for books written and/or illustrated by African-American authors about the African-American cultural experience), the Pura Belpré Award (for books written and/or illustrated by Latino/Latina authors about the Latino cultural experience), and the Mildred Batchelder Award (for books originally published in a foreign country and in a foreign language, translated and published by an American publisher). These lists provide an excellent resource for high-quality children's books for teachers to read for pleasure and for new material to use with their students.

Many of these books will be highlighted in children's book order forms. Instead of simply distributing the book orders and posting their due dates, teachers who are readers of these books will be able to talk about them and share their personal insights with their students. This is a wonderful way to provide students with an authentic literacy moment while distributing book order forms!

CULTIVATE YOUR OWN CURIOSITY

Teachers, like all adults, have questions about issues. They have a desire to learn about the world and bring that knowledge into their classroom. They also have hobbies and special interests. All of these needs are met through informational literature! While reading online articles about these topics is appropriate literate behavior, delving into informational books about them allows the reader to dig deeper into the topics or issues. By reading books related to special interests, new content, or personal hobbies, teachers will naturally cultivate both their curiosity and their reading habits.

Most book stores and libraries display artful arrangements of informational books—a very effective way to increase awareness of a variety of topics, authors, and new insights into a given hobby, leisure pursuit, or content area.

CONCLUDING THOUGHTS

Admittedly, these ideas for increasing the reading habit are not revolutionary. However, they all have one condition in common for success: they require intentionality. Teachers need to be cognizant of their need to nurture their personal reading lives. They need to be committed to making that happen. And they need to be diligent in their quest to read more books more often. All of these elements require intentionality.

When teachers see themselves as readers, they make the conscious effort to seek opportunities to read. In doing so, they have what it takes to promote the reading habit in their own students. They are not reading imposters; rather, they are readers. Their students see this, they understand that the teacher truly values literacy, and they will likely desire to read for pleasure on their own, just like their teacher!

REFERENCES

Applegate, A. & Mary D. Applegate (2004). The Peter effect: Reading habits and attitudes of preservice teachers. *The Reading Teacher, 57*, pp. 554–63.

Ruddell, R. (2005). *Teaching children to read and write: Becoming an effective literacy teacher* (4th ed.). Boston, MA: Allyn & Bacon.

Smith, F. (1988). *Joining the literacy club: Further essays into education.* Portsmouth, NH: Heinemann.

Chapter Two

Cultivating a Vibrant Classroom Library with Culturally Responsive Books

Who lives in your classroom? Often, early-elementary teachers lament their young students' assumptions that their teachers live in their classrooms. This question is not referring to this youthful naïveté, however. Rather, it is meant to inspire teachers to think beyond the obvious and delve into the affective climate they create in their classrooms through the words, insights, and values conveyed via the authors of the books housed in their classroom libraries (Gallagher, 2003). Likely, most K–2 teachers would reply, "Dr. Seuss, Ezra Jack Keats, Jan Brett," to name a few.

These are excellent authors, and their voices breathe life into elementary classrooms through the poignant messages their stories and illustrations convey. However, there are many lesser-known authors who have written insightful, thought-provoking children's books. Whose voices are heard? Whose voices are silenced by their absence? These are key questions to consider when building and replenishing a classroom library.

Teachers need to become acquainted with a wide variety of authors, those whose perspectives reflect their students' lived experiences and celebrate their culture (i.e., books as mirrors); and those whose perspectives provide new insights, beliefs, and values beyond their students' personal lives (i.e., books as windows). In other words, teachers must be intentional in their planning and include books that are authentic and culturally responsive to both their own classroom community and to the modern world. In doing so, the classroom's affective climate will convey respect, dignity, and validation for all cultures (Fleming, Catapano, Thompson, & Carrillo, 2016).

WHO LIVES IN YOUR CLASSROOM LIBRARY? SELECTING CULTURALLY RESPONSIVE LITERATURE

According to Gay (2000), culturally responsive teaching involves teaching beyond one's personal cultural experiences. It requires a mindset shift by classroom teachers to understand that all students do not learn the same way, see the world through the same lens, or relate to the same experiences. When teachers adopt a culturally responsive teaching stance, they begin to see their literature collections through a new lens, too.

All teachers should take time during the summer to review their classroom library and ask themselves: *Does my library provide a variety of culturally responsive texts for my students?* In order to answer this question, teachers will need to define "culturally responsive literature" for themselves. Hollie (2012) advocates for the inclusion of culturally *specific* books. He defines these as texts that "realistically tap . . . into the norms, mores, traditions, customs, and beliefs of the culture in focus" (p. 86).

Teachers can use the same characteristics of high-quality children's literature to assist in selecting books for their classroom libraries. In addition, however, the following questions will facilitate the effective evaluation of children's books regarding their authenticity as being responsive to the culture in focus (paraphrased from Fleming, et al., 2016).

- Does the author convey an insider's perspective to the cultural group?
- Are the illustrations free of cultural stereotypes?
- Is the language and dialog accurate to the culture?
- Are racial, gender, religious, and ethnic stereotypes avoided?
- Did the author share evidence of research for informational books?
- Are culturally diverse experts referenced and represented in informational books?
- Whose voices are heard in books about historical events, scientific discoveries, artistic achievements, etc.?

Tens of thousands of children's and young adult books are published each year (see ala.org/tools/number-children's-books-published). Needless to say, it is overwhelming to keep up with the most current information on quality children's literature. Several resources exist to assist teachers in keeping up to date on children's literature. Here are two exceptional websites:

- The American Library Association's website (ala.org) provides comprehensive lists of books for a variety of categories, most notably their award winners. The award lists are updated annually. The following awards target diverse authors and/or experiences: Pura Belpré Award (for Latino/Latina authors and illustrators); Coretta Scott King Award (for African-American authors and illustrators); Mildred Batchelder Award (for best translated work of children's literature); Schneider Family Book Award (for best book about the disability experience). The complete list of books, print, and media awards can be found at ala.org/awardsgrants/.

- The Cooperative Children's Book Center of the University of Wisconsin-Madison's website (www.ccbc.education.wisc.edu) is a resource "committed to identifying excellent literature for children and adolescents and bringing this literature to the attention of those adults who have an academic, professional or career interest in connecting young readers with books" (www.ccbc.education.wisc.edu/about/default.asp). This comprehensive website provides lists of multicultural literature, along with selection guidelines.

The Appendix provides a list of culturally diverse authors and their books written for beginning readers. This resource is intended to provide a variety of genres, authors, and cultural perspectives to assist elementary teachers in developing and evaluating their library collections. Additionally, this resource provides names of authors and illustrators whose voices need to be included in the classroom's library and integrated across the curriculum.

INCREASING ACCESS TO BOOKS IN YOUR LIBRARY: CREATING LITERACY MOMENTS WITH LITERATURE

Rejuvenating the collection of books contained in the classroom library is not effective if teachers do not intentionally promote its use throughout the day. If students are not reading the books, the library will be irrelevant. Teachers need to think creatively to construct a library that serves as an integral component to their students' daily literacy development. The classroom library must be a vibrant, interactive focal point of the classroom. Unless teachers intentionally develop opportunities for interacting with the books, students' access to them will be limited.

The function of a classroom library must be to provide access to quality literature for all students. This is not a new concept. For example, in 1928, Marie Staib posited,

> Why have a library in your classroom where it is accessible and companionable to students? Because it is accessible in the truest meaning of the word; alluring,

since it seems to actually beckon to the students; compelling to the scholar who does the thing when he cannot put it aside; and fascinating to him who will read a book that is recommended and offered without additional effort. (p. 762)

Fast-forward to 2000, when the International Reading Association (now the International Literacy Association) published its position statement on "Providing Books and Print Materials for Classroom and School Libraries" (IRA, 2000). The authors of this statement centered their stance around the importance of access to books. They noted that "children who have access to books are more likely to read for enjoyment, and thus increase their reading skills and their desire to read to learn" (n.p.). Without appropriate access to books, children may learn the skills necessary to read, but they will not likely develop the desire or habit of reading.

What does it mean to have access to books? Simply providing an attractive, well-organized classroom library isn't enough. Access entails providing time for, and contact with, reading during class time. This includes silent reading time, reading aloud from the library's collection, and selecting books to integrate across the curriculum. Teachers must know quality literature, their authors, *and* their students in order to make accurate recommendations that match children's interests with the content of the books. This is what authentic access to books looks like. It is meaningful. It is intentional. It is the foundation for creating and capitalizing on literacy moments.

Teachers should consider ways to motivate their students to interact with the books by creating innovative book displays and activities centered on engaging students in using their classroom library (Witter-Easley, 2015). Following are descriptions of ten creative ideas for increasing access to books by increasing students' interactions with literature contained in their classroom's library. This list is intended to set a foundation for teachers on which to build their own unique ideas for additional book displays.

- Dioramas, Dollhouses, and Playgrounds—Teachers will create a visual, either two- or three-dimensional display, in which various objects and pictures from specific children's books are inserted into the scene. For example, they could create a winter wonderland scene and insert specific book characters or key artifacts from books into the scene. Once it is completed, the teacher will number each object and create an answer key for students to use to guide them in matching up each item in the scene to its correlating book title. The teacher will need to display the books that go with each object around the scene for the students' perusal, and to help them find the objects in each book. This will likely pique their interest in a book they may not have otherwise selected.

- I Spy a Good Book—Modeled after Walter Wick's amazing photographic illustrations for Jean Marzollo's (1991) *I Spy: A Book of Picture Riddles*, and the numerous sequels, teachers create a collage of pictures based on themes, discipline-specific topics, or images from books contained in their classroom library. The students can contribute to a class poster by providing a picture and a clue, such as: "I spy a drawing tool used by Harold!" (Answer = purple crayon).

- Mystery Box Ballots—Teachers can display a mystery series for beginning readers, such as *Nate the Great* (Sharmat, 1972), *Clubhouse Mysteries* (Draper, 2011), *West Meadows Detectives* (O'Donnell, 2015), *Precious Ramotswe Mysteries* (McCall Smith, 2012), or *Pack-n-Go Girls Adventures* (Diller, 2013). They will read aloud one of the books to the class. Next, they'll pause at key moments in the book and have students make predictions about the mystery and place them in the "Mystery Box." Teachers should share the predictions during the read aloud and use the ideas to chart/graph possible solutions. The benefit of reading aloud from the first book in a series is that it creates a natural motivation for individuals to read other books in the series on their own.

- Read-Aloud Winners—Teachers can display four or five award-winning books that would be exciting read alouds. Students peruse the books and place in a ballot box their vote for the next read-aloud selection. At the end of a given period of time, the teacher announces the winner and reads it aloud to the class. This creates a vested interest in the students and empowers them as full participants in their classroom literacy environment. Furthermore, by having students skim the books on display, the teacher will likely motivate students to read the books they voted for during silent reading time (especially if they are disappointed that their choice did not win).

- Birthday Books—Each month, the teacher will create a colorful, celebratory display of books by authors whose birthdays fall during the month (see Appendix for a list of authors and their birthdates). They will challenge students to read several books by one (or more) of the authors on display. To encourage students' interaction with the books, teachers can place a sign-up sheet near the display for students to volunteer to either read aloud from one of the books, or to give the class a quick book commercial about one of the author's books.

- Art Books: Read with Purpose—For this display, teachers place several art activity books for early readers in a learning center, along with scrap paper, scissors, crayons, etc. They will bookmark pages with clearly written instructions and provide time for small groups to visit this center throughout the week. It is best to rotate various art books throughout the year: how-to-draw, collage projects, origami, recycled projects, etc. By using how-to books with beginning readers, teachers create opportunities for their students to realize that their reading skills serve a purpose. The Usborne Book Company™ publishes a wide variety of art activity books written for beginning readers with clearly written and illustrated step-by-step instructions.

- Nature Detectives—Teachers will display seasonal informational science books near a classroom window, along with basic detective supplies: magnifying lenses, sorting trays, paper, pencils, rulers, binoculars, etc. They will change the display to reflect the current season: leaf identification books for fall, snowflake informational books for winter, animal tracking or birdwatching books for spring. Teachers should encourage students to use the books as guides for their observational skills, as well as inspiration for learning more or completing various activities.

- Mystery Friend—Teachers can take student interest inventories to a new level of motivation! Each week, they could create a display of a "Mystery Student-of-the-Week." After reviewing the students' answers on his/her interest inventory, the teacher will assemble a set of books that pertain to his/her interests. They will then put the books together in an attractive display and give a brief booktalk early in the week. Throughout the week, teachers will allow students to write down guesses as to which classmate matches the books on display. They will reveal the mystery student at the end of the week and allow him/her to select one of the books for the daily read aloud.

- Arts-Based Book Displays—Teachers will assemble a still life that serves as both a creative art project and an authentic book display. First, they will arrange objects related to a current theme or disciplinary unit of study into a still life (an arrangement of various objects). Next, they will place corresponding books alongside the arrangement for students to explore. The information in the books will likely inform their drawing/painting of the still life, as well as encourage them to read interesting books they may have otherwise ignored.

- What Will I Be When I Grow Up?—There are many days on the calendar that serve to acknowledge and celebrate various professions. Teachers could choose two such days per month and create a book display in honor of those careers. For example, they might start the school year with displays for National Environmental Services Week (usually the second week in September), and National Farm and Ranch Safety and Health Week (third full week in September). They should display informational books, biographies, and other relevant genres (poetry anthologies related to these professions/topics). In addition to the books, teachers could post questions on a bulletin board for students to "read to find out," such as: What do you need to do to become an environmental scientist? How do farmers keep their animals safe and healthy? How do I become a rancher? Teachers will set aside time near the end of the display period to talk about what they learned from the books. This not only encourages students to read a variety of books, it conveys the teacher's expectation that through their literacy development the children will become college and career ready. An excellent resource for over 1,500 "National Days/Weeks" is www.nationaldaycalendar.com.

SILENT READING TIME

The hallmark of literacy development is the provision of time for students to sit and read continuous text. When teachers set aside time for students to select their own books and read freely for a designated period, they send a powerful message to their students: It is important to spend time reading. After all, we set aside time for what's important to us. We model authentic use of the classroom library every day by allowing students to find books to read independently. Unfortunately, sustained silent reading seems to have diminished as test-preparation time has increased during the school day. If we truly believe that our mission is to create lifelong readers, then teachers must intentionally set aside time to nurture that through uninterrupted, sustained silent reading.

To be truly effective, silent reading must not only be sustained for a specific period, it must also be united: everyone in the classroom participates at the same time. Too often, teachers assign silent reading as a "center" to be completed during small-group guided reading instruction time. However, beginning readers lack the self-discipline to remain focused for long periods of time, causing the teacher to stop his/her small-group instruction and redirect the students in this center. Instead, the following procedures are recommended for maximizing the power of silent reading time.

1. Everyone in the room participates at the same time. Each child selects a few books from the classroom library, finds a quiet place in the room, and enjoys their books.

2. Build reading stamina by starting out the year with five minutes of sustained silent reading time and gradually extend the time to fifteen minutes. This helps beginning readers to stay focused on reading, knowing that they won't have time to waste chatting with friends.

3. Allow kindergartners and first graders to bring a favorite stuffed animal from home (add it to their school supply list). Keep them in a special place near the classroom library. Develop the routine for silent reading time in which students find a quiet place in the room and whisper-read to their stuffed animal. This builds reading fluency, as well as develops their motivation to read during this special time.

4. The teacher reads, too! When the teacher sets aside time to read alongside the students, they receive the message that the teacher is a fellow reader. This creates a literacy community and cultivates everyone's reading habit.

5. The teacher should select a book from the classroom library to read independently at this time. While reading, s/he should demonstrably react to pertinent moments in the book (i.e., laugh aloud, gasp, etc.). This draws children's attention, often causing them to ask the teacher if s/he plans to read that book aloud. Once interest in the book has been created, instead of promising to read it aloud, the book could be placed on the whiteboard ledge with a sign-up sheet so students can sign up to read it on their own.

6. Develop a routine. Schedule silent reading at the same time each day so students can rely on it as a consistently important part of their day. One method is to set aside the first fifteen minutes after lunch recess. This allows students to know that when they return to the room, they should select their books and begin reading right away. It offers a gentle, developmentally appropriate transition from active play to focused classroom lessons. It is important to remain faithful to this time. If it is typically dropped from the schedule to accommodate special activities or events, the students receive the message that it isn't as important as other subjects or activities.

7. Try implementing an *unsilent* reading time. Periodically have students each select a book that they enjoy reading independently (without much assistance). Pair them up and have them take turns reading to each other while sitting together in a favorite spot in the classroom. This is an effective way to build reading stamina, develop their self-efficacy as readers, and nurture a literacy-rich community (see Figure 2.1).

Cultivating a Vibrant Classroom Library with Culturally Responsive Books   19

Figure 2.1. Two beginning readers enjoy a book together during an *unsilent* reading time.
Photo credit: J. Witter-Easley

Beginning readers may feel overwhelmed or frustrated by having to pick a book from the entire classroom library. This often manifests itself in statements such as: *I can't find anything to read.* To overcome this hurdle, teachers could plan ahead and provide the following literacy moments throughout the day:

- Booktalks—Teachers should set aside several moments each week to provide interactive booktalks. They will select several books from the classroom library that relate to a theme, genre, author, unit of study, special event, etc. Teachers could motivate students to read the books by focusing each talk on a key artifact related to it, such as a magnifying lens for a mystery book. Effective booktalks are those in which the teacher has read the books and truly enjoyed them. They should display the books from the talk so that students will successfully find them for use during silent reading time.

- How do readers choose books?—Teachers must take the time to teach this process through a think aloud: discuss reading purposes (enjoyment, information, persuasion). They could distribute interest inventories that ask students to articulate their personal hobbies, favorite subjects, etc. This will help them become aware of their thought processes. Teachers will create an anchor chart of these selection procedures and post it near the classroom library for reference throughout the year.

- Highlight new library acquisitions—If the classroom participates in catalog book order opportunities, the classroom teacher should use the arrival of the new books as a literacy moment by booktalking the new classroom books (usually free for the teacher based on a point system) and prominently displaying them as "New Books" near the classroom library.

TEACHER READ ALOUDS

An essential component of an early elementary classroom is teacher read alouds. When the teacher reads a book, article, or other authentic text aloud to the students, s/he offers many opportunities for developing their students' reading abilities. These benefits include, but are not limited to:

- Increasing students' vocabulary levels by exposing them to a wide variety of academic, creative, and interesting word choices used by authors.
- Enhancing students' experiences in reading new texts and hearing from new authors.
- Creating a literacy community by providing all students with a common literary experience so that each child and the teacher have a shared insight into the human condition.
- Allowing beginning readers to hear an expert reader (the teacher) approach a text with fluency, expression, and passion.
- Providing opportunities for the teacher to model through thinking aloud about a passage or moment of confusion so that beginning readers see how to monitor their thinking and apply fix-it strategies when comprehension breaks down.
- Engaging beginning readers in interactive discussions that promote critical thinking and interpretive meaning-making with their teachers and peers (Hoffman, 2011).
- Creating a literacy climate in which texts are celebrated, used as sources of information, and revered as integral components of our lives.

Teachers of all grade levels will enhance their students' literacy lives by taking the time to read aloud to them each day. This could take the form of reading for pleasure, enhancing a topic of discussion, adding insight into the human condition, setting the stage for learning about a specific concept, or infusing content areas with additional information outside of the assigned textbook. Teachers who read aloud for these, and many other purposes, will convey to their students that they truly see literacy as a key to knowledge development in all domains: social, emotional, intellectual, spiritual, relational, and psychological (to name a few). Following are suggestions for enhancing literacy moments through interactive read alouds.

- Poetry Breaks—Teachers should keep a few poetry anthologies on their desks so that they are readily available when moments present themselves for a poetry break. When students have completed an activity, are lined up and waiting for an event to begin, or are transitioning between subjects, teachers can take an anthology from their desk and read aloud several poems for the class to enjoy. In this way, teachers expose students to a genre of unique writing style for pure enjoyment. They signal to their class that writers use many formats to convey ideas. Furthermore, teachers convey to beginning readers that written language is beautiful and something to savor and celebrate.

- Make Eye Contact—It is important for teachers to think about their read alouds as opportunities to draw their students into the book. The most effective way to do this is to stand at the front of the room and hold the book open for all to see. While the teacher reads the words, s/he will also look at the class, making eye contact with individuals and displaying facial expressions, too. This may seem obvious, but with the increased use of document cameras during read-aloud time, it is necessary to highlight this key element of engaging students. When teachers rely on projecting the book on the screen, they tend to sit by the camera with their head down. This creates a sense of detachment between the students and the book and the teacher. So, save the document camera for follow-up discussions or word recognition activities.

- Keep the Students at their Desks—A popular read-aloud format seems to have arisen in many early elementary classrooms. It involves having students sit on the floor, gathered around the teacher as s/he sits in a rocking chair. The intention here is to create a cozy atmosphere, where children are closer to the teacher. However, a common issue that arises in this format is increased management concerns. The students begin to sprawl, invading their peers' "space," causing conflicts during the read aloud. Moreover, students seated near the back of the group tend to become distracted and chat with their neighbors. The teacher, trapped in the rocking chair, becomes frustrated and pauses the reading to manage these unwanted behaviors.

Alternatively, when the students remain in their desks, the teacher is free to walk around the room, using his/her proximity to limit unwanted chatter. The students' personal space is well defined, thereby avoiding any conflicts or disruptions. The teacher makes eye contact, reads expressively, and creates enthusiasm as s/he engages all students in the book.

CONCLUDING THOUGHTS

Teachers will cultivate their beginning readers' motivation by stocking the classroom library with culturally responsive books. To ensure quality, they should use selection criteria to determine which books to add to the collection so that all voices are heard. Once the classroom library is organized and filled with excellent books, the teacher needs to consider how to make the books accessible to his/her students. This is key to literacy development. Teachers must intentionally create literacy moments using the books in their libraries throughout the day for a variety of learning purposes.

There are several ways for teachers to motivate students to interact with the books in the library. For example, they could create vibrant book displays based on themes and authors. Here, teachers develop creative opportunities for students to interact with the books on display so that they will become interested in reading them on their own. Furthermore, when teachers consistently make time for both silent reading and reading aloud, they will easily integrate the classroom library's books into the daily lives of their students. The key here is consistency: teachers must set aside time each day for independent silent reading and for reading aloud across content areas. The suggestions for implementing these methods are intended to lay a foundation for teachers to build upon as they see their classroom library as an important source for creating literacy moments.

REFERENCES

Fleming, J., S. Catapano, C. M. Thompson, & S. Ruvalcaba Carrillo. (2016). *More mirrors in the classroom: Using urban children's literature to increase literacy*. Lanham, MD: Rowman & Littlefield.

Gallagher, K. (2003). *Reading reasons: Motivational mini lessons for middle and high school*. Portland, ME: Stenhouse.

Gay, G. (2000). *Culturally responsive teaching: Theory, research, & practice*. New York: Teachers College Press.

Hoffman, J. (2011). Coconstructing meaning: Interactive literary discussions in Kindergarten read alouds. *The Reading Teacher, 65*, 183–94.

Hollie, S. (2012). *Culturally and linguistically responsive teaching and learning: Classroom practices for student success*. Huntington Beach, CA: Shell Education.

International Reading Association. (2000). *Providing books and other print materials for classroom and school libraries: A position statement of the International Reading Association*. Newark, DE: International Reading Association.

Staib, M. (1928). A classroom library. *The English Journal, 17*(9), 762–65.

Witter-Easley, J. (2015). Bringing books to life: Revitalize your classroom library with interactive book displays. *Literacy Today*, July/August, 24–5.

CHILDREN'S BOOKS CITED

Diller, J. (2013). *Mystery of the ballerina ghost: Austria (Pack-n-Go Girls Adventures Vol. 1)*. Colorado Springs, CO: WorldTrek Publishing.

Draper, S. (2011). *The buried bones: Clubhouse Mysteries*. New York: Aladdin.

Marzollo, J. (1991). *I spy: A book of picture riddles*. New York: Scholastic.

McCall Smith, A. (2012). *The great cake mystery: Precious Ramotswe's very first case*. New York: Anchor Books.

O'Donnell, L. (2015). *The case of the snack snatcher: West Meadows detectives*. Toronto: OwlKids Books.

Sharmat, M. W. (1972). *Nate the great*. New York: Scholastic.

Chapter Three

Empowering Beginning Readers through Author Studies

Parents often ask teachers of beginning readers, *How can we help our children learn to read?* The best advice teachers can give is to tell parents to treat their young children like real readers. This involves a mindset shift for parents because rather than think of themselves as teaching reading lessons ("Time to review flashcards!"), this advice encourages parents to intentionally interact with their children as members of their reading community. When parents see their children as readers, they will convey this message to their children. Soon, their children will think of themselves as readers, rather than as students still learning to read.

Following this advice implies for parents their need to create literacy moments in their home life. One of the most powerful resources for providing these moments is found in the children's department of their local public library. By bringing their children to the library as part of their weekly routine, parents immerse their young readers in a literature-rich environment. They have a wide variety of picture books to select together. They can read these books to each other ("Wow, you are a very good reader!"), or they can take them home to read over and over again ("You read that book perfectly. Now read it to your baby brother/sister.").

Parents (and teachers) often feel overwhelmed when they approach their library's picture book section, however. Libraries organize these collections alphabetically by the author's last name. "Unless the parents and children are familiar with award-winning children's authors, they will not feel confident in selecting books that pertain to their interests, have been written in an engaging style, reinforce specific topical insights, or promote creativity" (Witter-Easley, 2012, p. 5). An effective way to empower parents, teachers, and subsequently, beginning readers, is to increase their knowledge of children's authors. Teachers can accomplish this by conducting author studies in the classroom.

THE BENEFITS OF AUTHOR STUDIES

Facilitating author studies provides benefits to beginning readers' literacy development in a variety of ways beyond simply helping parents to locate books at their local libraries. These benefits enhance both their skill development and their intrinsic motivation to read.

Skill Development

- Word recognition skills will be applied while reading the picture books.

- Vocabulary knowledge increases as children read books written by authors who do not prioritize using a controlled vocabulary for guided reading levels.

- Comprehension processes are developed and applied to authentic texts as teachers facilitate children's ability to make predictions, infer motives, draw conclusions, and guide readers through a variety of higher-level thinking skills.

- Oral reading fluency skills are nurtured as beginning readers read their books to one another, reread favorite passages, and read them to their families.

- Semantic processing is developed while beginning readers use context and syntax to determine unknown words, rather than solely relying on phonics and sight word knowledge.

Intrinsic Motivation Development

- Authentic texts provide a real purpose for reading because children understand that they are reading books from the real world (those found in books stores and in their local libraries).

- Sharing books by the same author creates interest in their topics as children read informational books and stories related to hobbies or special interests.

- Ability to self-select books creates a sense of empowerment. Beginning readers benefit from exercising their voice in selecting books to read.

When books by the same author are displayed and promoted in the classroom, children learn to discern which books to read by personal interests and tastes. They become active consumers of literature.

- Reading becomes a social event through the children's shared experiences of reading and discussing books by the same author. As the month progresses, students will begin to comment to one another about their favorite book by that author and they'll interact on a higher level regarding book recommendations and evaluative statements.

- Literacy moves beyond the classroom walls and into the children's world as they find the author's books in their public libraries and book stores. The act of reading becomes part of their lives, rather than simply completing a worksheet or an assigned reading in order to satisfy the teacher's requirements. They see books they've read in book stores, libraries, and doctor's waiting rooms. They develop personal favorites and may even ask for these books for presents.

SELECTING AUTHORS FOR BEGINNING READERS

There exists a plethora of wonderful children's picture book authors, representing all genres, including informational picture books and poetry collections. When determining which authors to study in K–2 classrooms, teachers should consider the following criteria.

1. *Focus on culturally and linguistically diverse authors.* Although thousands of books are published each year for children, only a small percentage of those books are written and/or illustrated by diverse authors. This means fewer books available to provide an insider's perspective on the issues, lifestyles, and experiences that are responsive and relevant to a given culture. Furthermore, providing access to books by diverse authors validates and elevates the culture for all students.

2. *Select authors and illustrators that have written and published several books.* Teachers will likely have their author study cover a month-long focus ("Author of the Month"). Therefore, studying an author of several books (at least five, ideally) will ensure that an assortment of books will be available to read and integrate into the curriculum throughout the month. Furthermore, when more books are accessible to students, they will have more opportunities to read them independently during silent reading time.

3. *Select living authors and/or illustrators.* In so doing, teachers will enhance their students' intrinsic motivation by creating opportunities for facilitating personal connections with the author, either through writing letters, emails, phone interviews, or video chats. The possibilities are endless!

4. *Select award-winning authors and illustrators.* Teachers can use award lists as their foundation for locating and selecting high-quality authors to study. These authors have met an award-granting organization's criteria for excellence, thereby establishing themselves as superior mentors for beginning readers and writers through their well-written and/or illustrated texts.

5. *Select authors and illustrators of both fiction and informational books.* When teachers intentionally select authors from a variety of genres, they ensure that their students interact with many forms of literature. They also provide all readers with access to books and authors representative of their personal interest levels. Finally, by introducing beginning readers to authors from many genres, teachers provide opportunities to increase their interests into new topics, hobbies, and pursuits.

ESTABLISHING A FRAMEWORK FOR CELEBRATING AN AUTHOR OF THE MONTH

Once teachers have selected their authors for each month of the school year, they'll need to develop a framework for effectively executing the program. Following are several elements that, when planned for, will ensure a positive experience for all.

1. *Take an inventory of the classroom library.* Teachers will need to determine the amount of each author's books they own. They should also decide on which books to order for multiple copies. School book clubs, thrift sales, resale shops, or community donations are excellent sources for multiple copies.

2. *Next, teachers must sort through the books* to select which they plan to integrate; to use for a creative activity; to read aloud for pleasure; to use for small-group lessons; or simply to have on hand for independent reading.

3. *Schedule a visit to the school library.* Teachers should meet with the librarians to enlist their help in acquiring a variety of books by the authors they plan to study. They can elicit their assistance in supporting their

program through creating library book displays, ordering extra copies, and guiding students toward choosing the books during their library time.

4. *Develop book displays.* Each month, teachers will create a display of the author's books, with a poster or bulletin board that celebrates the Author of the Month and creates interest in his/her books. Include bookmarks with lists of the author's titles. This will enable students to easily locate the author's books for independent reading time because they'll be in a central location. Additionally, teachers will have easy access to the books for their use during the day.

5. *Schedule author studies based on the month of their birthdays.* The "Author-of-the-Month" format is very conducive to selecting authors based on their birthdate. When following this format, teachers should schedule a special celebration on, or close to, the author's birthdate. In order to ensure that the students have sufficient background knowledge about the author's books, teachers will need to integrate their books and read them aloud throughout the month, especially leading up to the actual birthday celebration. This will help the students to appreciate the author's work and the creative activities the teachers have planned for the event. See the Appendix for a list of culturally diverse authors and illustrators organized by their birthday months, September through June.

SUGGESTIONS FOR CELEBRATING AUTHORS' BIRTHDAYS

Teachers who plan to integrate author studies into their curriculum and choose authors based on their birthdates will benefit from careful planning when it comes time to celebrate the author's birthday. The event should take on the feel of a birthday party, so teachers should plan to set aside this time for party games, activities, and general fun with their students. Following are key components to implement into the party plan.

Tell the Author's Story

Teachers will need to gather facts about the author's biography and develop a creative, party-oriented way to tell the story during the celebration. The best source for author biographical information is from the 300-plus volume series, *Something About the Author* (Gale Publications). This is available to schools and public libraries as an online resource (see www.gale.com/c/something-about-the-author-online).

Teachers will make this portion of the party most enjoyable when they package the information into an interesting storytelling event. For example, if the author writes poetry, tell their story in rhyming couplets. This has the added bonus of encouraging beginning readers to chime in with the rhyming word, which reinforces their understanding of onset and rime.

Another possibility is a photo album, in which the teacher locates images of the author's important places, hobbies, life events, etc. and puts them in a "scrapbook," turning the pages as the story is told. Teachers could try their hand at creating a "draw and tell" story, or a digital story set to songs that relate to the author's life. The possibilities are only limited by the teacher's creativity!

Take Time to Write to the Author

Instruct the students to create birthday cards, or participate in another authentic letter-writing activity. Encourage them to personalize their cards with favorite books or fun facts they learned about the author. Additional insights into this activity are described in the next section.

Plan Party Games Related to the Author's Books

The games could be traditional, such as "Pin the Mouse on the Elephant" (from *Seven Blind Mice* by Ed Young). BINGO cards with favorite characters, informational topics, etc. could be developed and used in a "Guess the character/topic" BINGO game.

Other games could be original ideas that connect directly to the books. These could be small group card games, dice games, guessing games, etc. Additional activities might be connected to outdoor fun, such as variations of tag games, chase games, or skill games. Regardless of the types of games developed for each party, the focus should be on having fun together and celebrating the author's books.

Set Aside Creative Time

Teachers could plan quick art projects or crafts for the party. Paper projects (such as paper bag character puppets, pop-up cards, basic paper-folding projects, etc.) provide a fun opportunity for creative expression without the stress of completing a more complex project or activity. Art projects that imitate a favorite illustrator's style are also appropriate and allow for exploration of various artistic techniques.

Sing "Happy Birthday, Dear Author!"

If the special author has a new book recently published, wrap it in birthday paper and open it dramatically after leading the students in singing "Happy Birthday" to the author. After the present is revealed, read it aloud to the class! Other ways to follow up the birthday song include: distributing special party favors (bookmarks, pencils, sticky note pads with an image of one of the author's story characters, small items related to informational books, etc.), or offering a special snack or treat (avoiding allergies and adhering to school policies, of course).

LITERACY MOMENTS WITHIN AUTHOR STUDIES

Through author studies, beginning readers will gain exposure to a wide variety of voices and perspectives while becoming personally acquainted with high-quality writers. Obviously, many benefits and literacy moments will occur as a result of this program. Following is a description of several impactful literacy moments that will naturally flow from time spent enjoying the works of children's authors and illustrators.

- *Book displays as gathering places for impromptu discussions*—When teachers create book displays each month for their celebrated author or illustrator, students naturally gravitate toward the books. While several students visit the display and peruse these books, literacy conversations ensue. These conversations range from general discussions of favorite books to recommendations for future reading. Children will likely ask one another about which books have been enjoyed the most and why they liked them.

    These moments seem natural, but they actually arise from carefully crafted displays and intentional selection of authors based on students' interests and the quality of their work. Teachers should eavesdrop on students when they gather at the display, so that they can nudge the conversations into these powerful literacy moments. When children discuss books in terms of personal reactions, reflective analysis, and individual insights, they become metacognitive thinkers about literature. They see themselves as integral members of a literate community!

- *Letters to and from the authors*—The reason for selecting living authors and illustrators as "Authors of the Month" is to set aside time during the birthday celebration to write to the authors. Teachers can develop creative writing formats based on the author's style (i.e., birthday poems for poets; murals that emulate an illustrator's artistic style; etc.). Once all the students have written their birthday greetings, teachers should collect them and write a cover letter explaining the program to the author. Next, teachers will put all the cards in an envelope, and include a letter-sized self-addressed, stamped envelope so the author can easily write back to the class. When teachers include the self-addressed envelope, they will most likely receive a "thank-you" letter from the author (along with posters or other promotional materials).

The author's "thank you" letter will become the class reading lesson that day! To capitalize on this as a literacy moment, teachers will make a copy of the letter for each student. To start the lesson, teachers will display the letter on the projector using the document camera. They'll first locate all the words the students have already learned (for Kindergarten and first graders, this will be basic sight words: the, I, am, you, like, etc.). This oral reading "rehearsal" is an important component to the beginning readers' success with reading the letter.

Next, the teacher will read the letter aloud, pausing for the students to read aloud the sight words they've already identified as they occur in the letter. The class will then join the teacher to chorally read the letter aloud. Teachers will lead the class in this oral reading activity several times to ensure fluency and confidence. Following the class choral reading activity, teachers will instruct their students to take turns reading their copies of the letter to a partner. Finally, teachers should tell the students to put the letters in their take-home folders to read aloud to their parents/caregivers. This is a very powerful, authentic literacy moment!

- *Bulletin boards with letters for geography connections*—As the response letters from authors arrive in the classroom, teachers can make connections to geography by creating a bulletin board with a map of the United States (or the world). They should title this, "Where in the World Do Our Favorite Authors Live?" After reading the letters aloud, teachers will post them around the perimeter of the map and use yarn to create a line that connects the letter to the author's home state. Informal discussions about the distance between the students' state and the author's will commence, offering opportunities for a variety of integrations across the curriculum.

    Additional activities based on this bulletin board include: comparisons (graphs) of miles traveled for each letter; student-made postcards with facts about the authors' home states; and student-made travel brochures containing information about famous birthplaces, state parks, geographic wonders, etc.

- *School Library Visits*—During weekly class trips to the school library, the teacher and librarian should collaborate to ensure that the current "Author of the Month's" books are on display so students can check them out. However, in addition to this, teachers should take time to review the names and types of books written by previously studied authors. This will empower beginning readers to use the library effectively because they will have a purpose in locating a book to check out.

  Instead of wandering around the library, aimlessly grabbing a book off the shelf before the time is up, beginning readers will purposefully walk toward the section that contains books within a specific alphabetic range, knowing their favorite author's last name and how to locate books shelved alphabetically by last names. Teachers' brief review of previously studied authors will provide a very impactful sense of power to young readers who have traditionally relied on adults to assist them in finding books at the library. Now, these beginning readers see themselves as consumers of literature, which will nurture their growing motivation to read for pleasure.

- *Author charts: math graphs*—One way to authentically integrate author studies across the curriculum is to create charts and graphs related to their work. Teachers can create graphs based on multiple-choice questions such as:

  Which book by this month's author is your favorite?
  Which of our authors have you enjoyed the most so far?
  Which of the following adventures would you like to see [name of series character] go on in a future book?
  Would you recommend this author to a friend?
  If you could choose the next Caldecott winner, which book by this month's illustrator would you choose?

  The graphs could be picture graphs, bar graphs, or pie charts. The possibilities are endless. Teachers should be sure to provide materials for students to use to fill in the graph. The materials should be of equal size (i.e., copies of class photos, rectangular stickers, sticky notes). This will ensure that the bar graphs and picture graphs accurately convey the true results because each bar, or set of pictures, will be created by items of the same size.

  Pie charts are most appropriate for answers based on two discrete choices. Teachers will need to supply two colors of equal-size pie pieces. They'll need to indicate which color should be used for which choice (i.e., red pie pieces = yes; blue pie pieces = no). Once students have clipped their wedges to a circular poster frame (cardboard pizza rounds work well), the teacher should make sure that each side of the pie consists of the same color—just like a real pie chart.

These graphs and charts promote numeracy and quantitative reasoning by guiding beginning readers through interpreting visually represented information. They also support literacy by having students read the questions, read the responses, and discuss them together during class time. Furthermore, when teachers leave the charts posted on the classroom walls, students will revisit the charts and talk to one another about their choices and compare ideas.

CONCLUDING THOUGHTS

There are many ways to facilitate beginning readers' literacy development, but when teachers infuse author studies into their curriculum, they promote development in areas of both skills and intrinsic motivation. Author studies ensure that students see their literate lives as more than discrete experiences of fluency, vocabulary, and word-recognition development. They see themselves as members of a literate society who discuss authors, share recommendations, and engage in critical analysis by comparing authors across writing styles and genres. In other words, they internalize the purpose of developing their reading skills so that they can participate in the ultimate purpose of reading: to engage with their peers and with authors through meaningful discussions that shape their ways of knowing about their world and themselves. This is time well spent!

REFERENCES

Witter-Easley, J. (2012). *Happy birthday, dear author!* Madison, WI: Upstart Books.

Part 2

Literacy Moments for Word Recognition and Vocabulary Development—An Introduction

Early elementary teachers need to teach students to recognize and read words using all of the domains of word recognition: phonics processes, orthographic processes, semantics, and syntax. Teachers reading this book will have learned the details of each of these processes in their college preparation courses. While the purpose of this book is not to provide an extensive description of each domain, a brief overview follows.

Given the fact that four domains for word recognition must be attended to, it's important to remember that decoding unknown words involves more than teaching phonics rules. Teachers must also attend to the development of semantic and syntactic processing. Semantic processing involves the use of context clues to determine the unknown word. Syntactic processing involves the use of sentence structure and grammatical knowledge to determine the unknown word. Both processes require beginning readers to understand that the text they're reading conveys meaning and must make sense, both contextually and grammatically. Throughout Chapters 4, 5, and 6, readers will find examples of using connected text from culturally relevant sources to assist them in creating literacy moments that develop the skill of using context and grammar to determine unknown words.

Many texts written for beginning readers may be too brief, however, to rely solely on context clues. One of the most effective word recognition processes for expanding beginning readers' repertoire of decoding is found in orthographic processing. This refers to using consistent spelling patterns within words to decode them. Teachers will instruct readers to notice the onset of a word—the initial consonant or consonant blend before the first vowel within a syllable. They will also instruct readers to learn word families, or the rime of a word. This entails several letters consisting of the first vowel and the following consonants within a syllable.

For example, in the word "track" readers will find two consistent and reliable spelling patterns: the onset and rime. Here, the onset is the /tr/ blend and the rime is /-ack/. So, rather than having beginning readers assign a sound to each letter where they would read this as: /t/ /r/ /a/ /c/ /k/, teachers better serve their students by having them notice that when they see /tr/ it will always be a one-breath blend of both sounds. And, more powerfully, when they see the rime /ack/ they will always know that it is two sounds together: /ak/. Now, they are sounding out the word as: /tr/ /ack/; this is much more efficient!

Furthermore, they will be able to generate new words with the same rime, such as: back, crack, jack, sack, black, snack, shack, etc. This is much more empowering for developing independence in beginning readers' literacy development than solely attending to the letter-sound relationships of phonics rules. Throughout these chapters, readers will find references to onsets and rimes found in poems, jump rope rhymes, song lyrics, and other authentic, culturally relevant texts.

Finally, in these next three chapters readers will find methods for intentionally creating literacy moments that foster vocabulary development. This is a key component of literacy development because vocabulary serves as a bridge between word recognition and comprehension. As Stanovich (1986) so aptly pointed out in his seminal work, readers who have a large vocabulary will be motivated to read more books, will know more words, and will be able to most successfully utilize semantic and syntactic processing skills to figure out unknown words.

Conversely, readers who do not have an extensive foundation of word knowledge will have increased difficulty in reading new texts because they will have fewer words to scaffold them when encountering unknown words. They will see themselves as ineffective readers, and will likely not choose to read for pleasure. This will cause them to continue to struggle because they will be exposed to fewer words than their reading peers. Therefore, a variety of activities that intentionally address vocabulary development and the acquisition of new words are included in each of these chapters.

It is my intention to have Chapters 4, 5, and 6 build on the foundation of the first three chapters. Here, readers will find methods and techniques for using their culturally responsive classroom libraries and print-rich environments to create literacy moments that attend to the development of beginning readers' word recognition and vocabulary processes. These chapters focus on framing these reading skills within the authentic context of culturally responsive materials, social justice topics, and the arts. When teachers create a learning community filled with authentic materials, they will find that many opportunities arise that will enable them to create literacy moments for nurturing the foundational skills of word recognition and vocabulary development.

REFERENCES

Stanovich, K. (1986). Matthew effects in reading: Some consequences of individual differences in the acquisition of literacy. *Reading Research Quarterly, 22,* 360–407.

Chapter Four

Immersing Students in a Print-Rich "Literacy Moments" Environment

Beginning readers are busy people. They work hard in school: learning how to decode text, solving complex math problems, completing seatwork activities, and developing their social skills with new friends and teachers. They play hard, too: expending great energy at recess and physical education class, participating in after-school sports leagues, and getting together with new friends on weekends. So, how do we set aside time for literacy moments given our students' jam-packed classroom schedules? How do we create an environment conducive to capitalizing on literacy moments throughout the school day?

The physical space of a learning community contributes significantly to the students' academic success in developing their literacy skills. Early elementary teachers realize the need to create a classroom environment that promotes beginning literacy skills so that their students will be immersed in print. In so doing, these teachers convey to their students that words are everywhere and the ability to read words will open up opportunities to learn new information, communicate their ideas, and nurture their curiosity about their world. Teachers who create print-rich classroom environments empower their beginning readers!

The print-rich physical domain entails more than putting up labels for items around the room, however. To create a learning community that is prepared to nurture and capitalize on literacy moments, teachers need to leverage a variety of elements within their classrooms. These elements include both the materials available for developing this type of learning environment, as well as the classroom's community of learners and their natural curiosity about the world of print. This curiosity can and should be cultivated from the first day of school.

ESTABLISHING A PRINT-RICH CLASSROOM BY CREATING CURIOSITY AMONG BEGINNING READERS

At the beginning of the school year, many teachers create a beautiful print-rich environment with commercial products such as posters, signs, learning-center labels, and word cards displayed on permanent fixtures (i.e., "clock" word card taped to the bottom of the classroom wall clock). Early-elementary students enter these rooms on the first day of school, marveling at the colorful environment and eager to see their friends and unpack their shiny new school supplies. This is a wonderful classroom environment, but what if teachers viewed the first week of school as a literacy moment and omitted the posters, labels, and word cards?

Instead, as they acquaint their new students with their learning environment, the teachers should lead their new students on a tour of the room, with blank word cards and thick, colorful markers in hand. This generates interest and curiosity, because the beginning readers will see that they are about to embark on important work. Their teacher has notecards and markers. S/He seems to need their assistance!

As the teacher leads the students to the writing table, for example, s/he shows them the bins for paper, cups for pencils, shelf for reference books, etc. Next, the teacher takes out a blank word card and says, "This is our writing table, so let's write that on our card here. That way, we'll always remember." Then, as the teacher prints *wr*, s/he says the sound of this consonant digraph, then *i*, *t*, and *ing*. This continues for the next word: *table*. Finally, the teacher tapes the word card along the side of the table and leads everyone in reading it aloud. Naturally, the teacher should follow the same procedure for the *pencil cup* and the *paper bin*, etc.

This is how teachers create an authentic literacy moment! Here, the beginning readers are immersed in the work of real reading and writing. Furthermore, because they helped in creating the labels for the room, they own that information. It belongs to them. This simple shift in creating a print-rich environment enables beginning readers to see themselves as literate members of the classroom. They will read the labels on their own throughout their days in school, rather than going to the writing table because they know its function but have no real sense of what the label says or means. When a new friend joins their classroom community, they will proudly read the signs and guide the student through their daily routines and centers.

MEANINGFUL PRINT IN THE CLASSROOM

The key to effectively establishing a print-rich environment that promotes beginning readers' literacy development is to ensure that the print is meaningful to the students. They need to witness its creation, provide oral language to assist the teacher in writing the information, and understand its context within their learning community. The following types of meaningful print are important in the development of word recognition and increased vocabulary. Through these visual language charts, teachers will be able to capitalize on a variety of literacy moments.

Oral Language Narratives (Morning Messages & Language Experience)

The act of having beginning readers dictate sentences to their teacher, who records their words on chart paper, is a tried-and-true practice in many early elementary classrooms (Labbo, 2005). Two of the most popular forms of this technique are Morning Messages (Graves, 1994) and Language Experience Approach (Stauffer, 1970). The key to a successful oral language narrative activity, however, is to construct it with the children so they are witnesses to the writing process, they are contributors to the written text, they see the process involved in writing the text, and they develop skills in generating ideas for writing a story or informational document (Wasik & Hindman, 2011).

Teachers can use traditional materials (chart paper and markers) or type them up on their computers while projecting them on their smartboard screen. Both formats offer their own sets of benefits. Traditional chart paper allows the teacher to model the formation of letters, for the youngest beginning readers. The computer-generated document can be printed and distributed to the students to read to their partners, and taken home to read to their parents. Since both formats provide excellent literacy moments, teachers should vary their technique and determine the best formats for a given narrative activity.

- *Morning Messages*—These oral language narratives provide beginning readers with a powerful routine to begin each school day. Typically, the teacher starts each message with a sentence that states the date: *Today is Monday, September 12*. Next, the teacher randomly selects the name of a child in the class, who then comes forward and dictates a sentence about the weather, an upcoming event, or a special activity for that day. After the student dictates his/her sentence, the teacher writes it on the chart paper, reading aloud each word as it is written. The whole class then chorally reads the message aloud.

  A second child is selected to dictate a sentence, and the process continues. After three children have had turns, the whole class chorally reads the entire message aloud. Because they have previously read the earlier sentences, they are building fluency in their repeated readings of the text. The benefits of this activity include: (a) exposing beginning readers and writers to the writing process, (b) allowing them to understand that words on the page represent their talk written down, (c) modeling for them the use of punctuation, capitalization, sentence structure, and (d) applying spelling and phonics rules to written text.

- *Language Experience Approach*—This narrative operates in a similar manner. The difference here is that this activity generally follows some source of stimulus, such as: field trips, guest speakers, classroom activities, current events, interesting stories, etc. Once the special event or activity has concluded, the teacher leads the students in dictating sentences related to their reactions, favorite parts, the sequence of events, etc.

Literacy Moments with Oral Language Narratives

For example, after the morning message has been completed and read aloud, the teacher spends several minutes making references to words containing a phonics rule they've recently practiced. These references can become "I notice" activities: "I notice that the words *today* and *play* both use the /ay/ family to make a long /a/ sound. Can you find other words in our message that used these letters to make the long /a/ sound?" The teacher then uses a brightly colored marker to underline the vowel digraph /ay/ in each word.

Comprehension counts, too! Whether composing a morning message or a language experience, teachers should also take time to discuss the text by asking questions about their sentences ("What do you think will happen during gym class today?"), and guiding them to think critically ("Why do you suppose that happened on our field trip?"). When they do so, their students learn that their narratives are not static documents. Rather, they'll see themselves as important contributors to the texts used for the work and activity of their classrooms.

Word Walls and Charts

Often, early elementary classrooms contain lists of words: weekly spelling lists, alphabetized sight word lists, word walls containing specific phonics rules, etc. These lists provide important information to the success of beginning readers. However, rather than post lists that are decontextualized from authentic experiences, teachers should look for meaningful opportunities and texts as the sources of creating and using these word charts with their students.

Word walls are most effective when they are generated from a reading experience, or to serve a real literacy purpose. So, instead of having an alphabetized assortment of words posted on the classroom walls on the first day of school, teachers should look for opportunities on which to intentionally capitalize throughout all content area classes for creating word walls with their students. Shifting this format from a teacher-centered approach to a shared approach will effectively engage beginning readers in actively using the word walls independently.

Word charts are developed with the students as a book is being read aloud, or in response to an experience in the classroom. These are not narratives, because they do not contain connected sentences, rather they are lists of words that are similar based on a phonics rule, spelling pattern, or content area theme. The key to success here is the co-creation of the chart with the students. If the teacher has already prepared a colorful word chart and plans to simply read through the list, the students will be disengaged and the chart will become classroom wallpaper.

Literacy Moments with Word Walls:

1. Read alouds and word charts go together! As a teacher previews a book for use as a read aloud, s/he will attend not only to the plot or informational content, but also to the author's word choices. Does the author use several words that follow a spelling pattern the class has been practicing? If so, plan to spend time after the read aloud having the students go back and listen for and locate those words. As the students find them, the teacher records them on chart paper, perhaps using two marker colors: one to highlight the spelling pattern, the other for the remaining letters in each word.

   At the conclusion of the book, the teacher will lead the students in a choral reading of each word on the list. Next, the students will turn to a friend and see if they can think of additional words with the same spelling pattern to add to the list. The teacher leads the whole class in listening to their peers' ideas and adding their words to the list. If a word sounds like it should be on the list, but doesn't actually follow the spelling pattern (a very common occurrence in the English language), teachers should write the word on the whiteboard and discuss why it wouldn't fit the criteria for the word chart.

   This literacy moment will continue beyond the class session when teachers adhere the chart to the wall at their students' eye-level. They should then use Velcro™ tape, placing a strip on the wall next to the chart and a matching strip on the side of a marker, adhering the marker next to the chart for the students' use. The students can now add to the word chart during their independent reading, with the teacher's encouragement to add new words with the spelling pattern as they find them in their own books.

2. Content areas are ripe for vocabulary charts! While much of the day in an early elementary classroom is focused on teaching children how to read, teachers need to remember that content areas are excellent sources of literacy moments, too. Informational books and textbooks in the areas of social studies, science, and mathematics contain disciplinary words that students will need to apply to their development of content knowledge.

Graphic organizers of informational text are excellent ways to create word charts in these content areas. For example, when studying a concept, put the main vocabulary word in the middle of a large sheet of unlined chart paper. Circle the word and draw lines like spokes in a bicycle wheel. At the opposite end of each line/spoke, write a topic related to the main word and generate lists of words from their text that pertain to this topic.

Continue this process as the unit of study progresses, adding new information and vocabulary words to the graphic organizer and rereading previously learned words along the way. When teachers co-create these graphic organizers with their students, they foster literacy development in several ways.

First, they model the process of determining importance of content information. As content is read aloud, the teachers pause and ponder in front of their students, demonstrating how they decide whether the information is important enough to include on their chart.

Second, and perhaps most importantly, they elevate their students' status from passive learners to content authorities who have valuable ideas to contribute to the classroom. This subtle, yet very powerful, benefit enables fledgling readers to see themselves as members of a literate community. Furthermore, they will interact with these graphic organizers for authentic purposes.

POETRY AND RHYMES

Early-elementary classrooms can be exciting hubs of learning when teachers seek fun, authentic ways to enhance their students' literacy development. Poetry and verses, such as jump-rope rhymes and playground chants, are excellent sources for creating such a learning environment. In addition, they provide rich language and rhythmic text from which to learn foundational skills in literacy.

Poems Written for Beginning Readers

These poems are very beneficial because their authors integrate basic sight words with interesting vocabulary to create rhythm and engage early elementary students in reading their poems. The rhyming words provide practice in identifying and reading words with similar onsets (the initial consonant or consonant blend in a syllable) and rimes (the first vowel following the initial consonant or consonant blend in a syllable).

Jump-rope Rhymes and Playground Chants

These culturally responsive texts are drawn from students' authentic experiences. While a variety of resources containing such rhymes are available to teachers, they will heighten their students' interest in these rhymes when they simply ask them to recite a favorite rhyme and dictate it to the teacher. In so doing, teachers elevate and validate their students' cultural experiences. As Ladson-Billings (1995) so succinctly stated, "Culturally relevant teachers utilize students' culture as a vehicle for learning" (p. 161). That being said, here are a few excellent resources to get teachers started in bringing jump-rope rhymes and chants into their classrooms:

Cole, J. (1989). *Anna Banana: 101 jump-rope rhymes.* New York: William Morrow & Co.
Cole, J. & Calmenson, S. (1993). *Six sick sheep: 101 tongue twisters.* New York: William Morrow & Co.
Dotlitch, R. K. (2004). *Over in the pink house: New jump rope rhymes.* Honesdale, PA: Boyds Mills Press.
Hague, M. (1993). *Teddy bear, teddy bear: A classic action rhyme.* New York: William Morrow & Co.
Opie, I. & Opie, P. (1992). *I saw Esau: The schoolchild's pocket book.* Cambridge, MA: Candlewick Press.

Literacy Moments with Poems and Rhymes

1. Poems have many "rimes"! Once the teacher has selected a poem from an anthology written for beginning readers, s/he will copy it onto lined chart paper in the same format. This can be done prior to its use in the classroom. The teacher reads the poem aloud and then has the students identify any words they would have already learned to read. Children can circle them on the chart. Next, the teacher and students chorally reread the poem, with the teacher pausing for the students to take the lead on the circled words.

    The teacher now references rimes (word families) within words at the end of verses by highlighting them in a different color (for example, cl**ock** and d**ock**). A new sheet of chart paper is posted and the teacher leads the class in reading these words, and brainstorming a list of additional words containing the same rime of /ock/. Again, this word chart is adhered to the classroom wall at a level at which the students have access to adding new words as they encounter them in their independent reading, etc.

2. Seasonal poems are excellent sources of topical vocabulary! Here, the teachers would follow the same procedure as described above, with the addition of highlighting seasonal words. They would then create a graphic organizer containing those words for students' reference during writing workshop. Individual or pairs of students could illustrate each word and post it on the chart. They'll now have a handy seasonal picture dictionary posted on their classroom wall.

3. Celebrate all students' cultures through their rhymes and chants! After teachers have successfully encoded the children's dictated rhyme onto chart paper, it's important to take time to have the students lead the class in the choral reading. If clapping is involved, teachers need to be sure to include it and any other rhythmic movements the children integrate into the rhyme or chant. This should be fun; it is a time to share and celebrate cultures together! Finally, the teacher uses the chant to reinforce new vocabulary as well as word identification concepts, such as onset and rime, blends, digraphs, etc. As with all print created in the classroom, these rhymes and corresponding word charts should remain on the classroom wall for use as a reference tool in both reading and writing.

SOURCES OF POEMS AND RHYMES FOR BEGINNING READERS

While a variety of leveled books and online sources are available to teachers, it is important to use poems written by children's authors whose work can be found in local libraries and book stores. This will convey to the students that they are real readers and they're reading poems from books that are found in the real world—not the sterile world of school and textbooks. Therefore, the following references are excellent sources of poems for beginning readers.

Poetry Anthologies:

deRegniers, B. S., Moore, E., White, M. M., and J. Carr (Eds.). (1988). *Sing a song of popcorn: Every child's book of poems*. New York: Scholastic.

Prelutsky, J. (Ed.). (1989). *Poems of A. Nonny Mouse*. New York: Alfred A. Knopf.
Prelutsky, J. (Ed.). (1983). *The Random House book of Poetry*. New York: Random House.
The Real Mother Goose. (1944). New York: Checkerboard Press.

Poet's Collections:

Adoff, A. (2000). *Touch the poem*. New York: Blue Sky Press.
Greenfield, E. (1991). *Night on Neighborhood Street*. New York: Picture Puffins/Penguin Books.
Grimes, N. (2001). *A pocketful of poems*. New York: Clarion Books.
Hoberman, M. (1991). *Fathers, mothers, sisters, brothers: A collection of family poems*. New York: Puffin/Penguin Books.
Hoberman, M. (2001). *You read to me, I'll read to you: Very short stories to read together*. Boston, MA: Little Brown.
Kuskin, K. (2003). *Moon, have you met my mother?* New York: HarperCollins.
Lewis, J. P. (1990). *A hippopotamusn't*. New York: Trumpet Books.
Milne, A. A. (1992). *Now we are six!* New York: Puffin Books.
Prelutsky, J. (1977). *It's Halloween*. New York: Scholastic.
Prelutsky, J. (1983). *It's Valentine's Day*. New York: Scholastic.
Prelutsky, J. (1986). *Ride a purple pelican*. New York: Greenwillow.
Prelutsky, J. (1984). *The new kid on the block*. New York: Greenwillow.
Sendak, M. (1962). *Chicken soup with rice: A book of months*. New York: Scholastic.
Silverstein, S. (1981). *A light in the attic*. New York: Harper & Row.
Silverstein, S. (1974). *Where the sidewalk ends*. New York: Harper & Row.
Stevenson, R. L. (1966). *A child's garden of verses*. Oxford: Oxford University Press.

CREATING IMPROMPTU LITERACY MOMENTS WITH YOUR PRINT-RICH ENVIRONMENT

Many teachers have experienced the following scenario: The school has a special assembly planned, or a guest speaker to visit the classroom, etc. The students are either lined up and ready to go, or sitting quietly in their seats waiting for the guest to arrive. Unfortunately, the guest is running late. What to do with the students during this five-minute gap? When teachers have created a print-rich environment, they have prepared many options for effective use of this valuable time: true literacy moments!

Following are descriptions of word games that teachers can implement when these last-minute opportunities arise. As teachers become more intentional and immersed in a "literacy-moments mindset," they will become quite adept at creating many more interactive word games.

Whiteboard Word Wonders

Teachers can quickly turn their whiteboard space into a game board for the whole class to use with these word games:

- Mystery Word: Teachers draw a 3 × 3 grid on the whiteboard. Next, they call on nine different students to each pick a word from one of the word walls on display. They can then print them in one of the nine spaces on the grid. Next, the teacher gives a clue as to which word s/he is NOT thinking of, so that when the students guess that word, it is crossed off. The last remaining word is the mystery word (see Table 4.1).

Table 4.1. Mystery Word

cake	summer	sleep
box	frog	state
book	the	today

- Clues:

    "It is NOT a word that rhymes with 'keep'." (Students say, "sleep" and teacher makes an "X" over the word.)
    "It is NOT a word with a long /a/ and silent /e/." (Cross out "cake".)
    "It is NOT a sight word." (Cross out "the".)
    "It is NOT one of the four seasons." (Cross out "summer".)
    "It is NOT a word that starts with the same sound as 'stone'." (Cross out "state".)

    Play continues, with students making predictions as to which word it will be, until the mystery word is revealed at the end.

- Vocabulary Builder: This idea is based on Janet Allen's (1999) strategy of "linear arrays" (p. 52). The teacher writes a vocabulary word on the board, then places three empty word spaces next to it in a row. Finally, after the third empty space, the teacher writes an antonym of the vocabulary word. The students' task is to think of a word for the first empty space that is a synonym for the vocabulary word, only a slight gradation from the original. They do the same for the next two spaces, but each next word's meaning should lean away from the original word's meaning and gradually shift in meaning toward the antonym. This is an effective game for reviewing content area topics posted on word charts (see Table 4.2).

Table 4.2. Vocabulary Builder

| SOLID | | | | LIQUID |
|---|---|---|---|---|//
| | | | | |

Students should turn to a friend and brainstorm ideas for the first box. Teachers will need to scaffold this so that they have students come up with words one box at a time. That will help visual learners to participate because they will see the previous word and it will enable them to think of a word that is a shade different from it. So, in the first blank box, students may suggest "sturdy," or "hard," or "cold," etc. The teacher should list all the suggestions below the space/box and have the class come to agreement on which word they believe fits best in that box. Then move onto the next box. Continue until the last space has a word that would relate to "liquid" such as "melt," or "heat."

- I Spy a Word: Using the variety of word walls and vocabulary charts on display, the teacher silently picks one of the words and tells the class, *I spy with my little eye, a word that [rhymes with], [starts with], [is the opposite of], etc.* The students must quickly raise their hands, or whisper to a partner to share their answers. If more than one word fits the description, the teacher lists all of the students' answers on the board and discusses them.

  Another variation of this game is to draw lines on the board, one per letter in the word, and slowly begin to spell the word, first filling in the initial letter, pausing for guesses, then the next letter, etc., until the word is either correctly guessed or spelled in full. This is similar to "Rivet" (Cunningham, Hall, & Cunningham, 2000, p. 70), a vocabulary game that focuses on key words from either fiction or informational text.

- Word Wonders: Point to a word from one of the word lists and print it on the whiteboard. Then, tell the class to take turns spelling the word to their neighbor. Next, tell them to spell the word as a plural (if it is a noun). If the word is a verb, challenge them to spell the word in past tense. Next, they must think of an antonym of the word and spell it to their partner. Continue with synonyms. Follow up each spelling challenge by printing the correct answers so that all students will learn both the oral and visual forms of each word.

- Friends' First Letters: Keep individual copies of students' class photos on hand. Hold up the photo of one of their classmates and challenge them to read a word from the word wall that starts with the same letter of this friend's first name. List these words on the board as the students read them aloud. For students whose names begin with a consonant digraph or blend, be sure to challenge the class to only locate and read words with the same digraph or blend.

CONCLUDING THOUGHTS

Print-rich environments are integral to the nurturing of beginning readers' word recognition processes and vocabulary development. Teachers must go beyond simply posting commercial posters and charts on the classroom walls. Instead, they need to intentionally seek opportunities to involve their students in the creation and use of these charts. This includes all modes of classroom print: oral language narratives, word walls, graphic organizers, labels, and lists. When teachers invite students into the process of creating and using environmental print, they create curiosity in the literacy process and demonstrate that the purpose for learning to decode words is to comprehend connected text.

Finally, once teachers create a vibrant print-rich learning community, they can leverage these visual texts for impromptu literacy moments. Word games and engaging activities will encourage students to apply their decoding skills to authentic purposes. They will increase their vocabulary base and cultivate their strategies for using context clues to identify and define unknown words. These benefits reside in the overall power of learning to read using culturally responsive and relevant texts—both from published works and from children's cultural experiences.

REFERENCES

Allen, J. (1999). *Words, words, words: Teaching vocabulary in grades 4–12*. York, ME: Stenhouse.

Cunningham, P., Hall, D. P., & Cunningham, J. W. (2000). *Guided reading the four-blocks way*. Greensboro, NC: Carson-Dellosa Publishing.

Graves, D. (1994). *A fresh look at writing*. Portsmouth, NH: Heinemann.

Justice, L. M., Kaderavek, J. M., Fan, X., Sofka, A., & Hunt, A. (2009). Accelerating preschoolers' early literacy development through classroom-based teacher-child storybook reading and explicit print referencing. *Language, Speech, and Hearing Services in Schools, 40*, 67–85.

Labbo, L. D. (2005). From morning message to digital morning message: Moving from the tried and true to the new. *The Reading Teacher, 58*, 782–85.

Ladson-Billings, G. (1995). But that's just good teaching! The case for culturally relevant pedagogy. *Theory into Practice, 34*(3), 159–65.

Stauffer, R. G. (1970). *The language-experience approach to the teaching of reading*. New York: Harper & Row.

Wasik, B. A., & Hindman, A. H. (2011). The morning message in early childhood classrooms: Guidelines for best practices. *Early Childhood Education, 39*, 183–89.

Chapter Five

Integrating Popular Culture to Facilitate Foundational Literacy Skills

The ultimate purpose in literacy development is to create lifelong learners who are empowered to critically analyze information and question the norms of their world. When teachers engage in social justice literacy development for their beginning readers, they will integrate cultural content into their curriculum. This means that teachers will intentionally seek out "alternative discourses [that] represent peoples' lived realities and their essential understandings about their world" (Compton-Lilly, 2003, p. 22). According to Gloria Ladson-Billings (1995), "students must develop a broader sociopolitical consciousness that allows them to critique the cultural norms, values, mores, and institutions that produce and maintain social inequities" (p. 162). One way early-elementary teachers can accomplish this is by intentionally integrating popular culture into their curriculum. This includes the fun, artistic, and unique elements as well as current social justice issues relevant to their students' experiences and developmental level.

What is culture? According to the Merriam-Webster dictionary, culture is defined as "the customary beliefs, social forms, and material traits of a racial, religious, or social group; *also*: the characteristic features of everyday existence (such as diversions or a way of life) shared by people in a place or time" (www.merriam-webster.com/dictionary/culture). From this comprehensive definition, culturally responsive teachers have a wealth of material available to them for literacy moments. When teachers use authentic materials that connect cultural realities of "everyday existence" it follows that they will delve into social justice issues.

Children of all ages see and feel and live and breathe the daily events of their homes, their neighborhoods, their families, and their communities. Teachers honor their students' experiences when they integrate cultural artifacts as tools for learning. Doing so "creates an environment that fosters humanity" (Ahmed, 2018, p. 2). Teachers who incorporate a humanizing pedagogy into their daily classroom experiences provide their students with a culturally relevant curriculum (Bartolomé, 1994; Ladson-Billings, 1992). Beginning readers who have access to such materials will become intrinsically motivated to apply their newly learned foundational reading skills to these texts because they are meaningful and they validate and elevate their cultural experiences.

When teachers use authentic, culturally responsive texts to teach their beginning readers across all content areas, they create opportunities to apply a variety of word recognition processes to the reading. This is accomplished because the text is meaningful, and the students will seek to read it to construct meaning and comprehension. Therefore, the use of these texts will not only convey the importance of applying phonics and skills and orthographic knowledge to decode words. Rather, students will need to develop their ability to use semantic processes by relying on their understanding of the text to use context clues when they come to an unknown word. This is also true for applying syntax processes: the students will need to understand the sentence structure and grammatical context and use that information to assist them in solving an unknown word.

WHAT IS YOUR OPINION? USING GRAPHS TO PROMOTE LITERACY SKILLS

Children are immersed in the realities of their world, their communities, their cultural artifacts, and their families and friends. Teachers of beginning readers can harness these realities and provide authentic opportunities for their students to practice their word recognition skills by creating thoughtful questions for the students to respond to on a large graph.

When teachers post a culturally relevant question on chart paper and lead the class in chorally reading it aloud, they are conveying to their students that print serves a purpose. Teachers can demonstrate that unknown words can be decoded and defined by using context clues and sentence structure. Their students see reading as meaningful and socially important. After all, they need to apply their reading skills so that they can decode the graph's question and mark their response to accurately convey their opinions.

The graphs need be constructed with care. Teachers can ask spontaneous questions, but they must remember that their graph will model proper letter formation, punctuation, and grammatical rules. In addition, the printing should be large enough to read from across the room. In order to ensure that the students can respond to the question and later use quantitative reasoning

Integrating Popular Culture to Facilitate Foundational Literacy Skills 53

Figure 5.1. Sample bar graph created with similar-sized markers.
Photo credit: J. Witter-Easley

to discuss the results, teachers will need to provide all students with equally sized and shaped response tokens, such as copies of individual student photos, stickers, or stamps. For example, when using photos, students will paste their pictures in the row or column next to their desired response, thereby forming a bar graph for ease in mathematically interpreting the class results. Finally, teachers will make their graph colorful and interesting to look at (see Figure 5.1).

Culturally Relevant Graph Questions

Teachers should construct questions that grow out of shared class experiences: books read together, informal conversations, seasonal events, etc. One way for teachers to establish relationships with their students outside of class instruction is to sit with them during lunch time. Here is where authentic conversations happen, and both the teacher and students get to know each other as real people. There are no lesson plans to cover, no instructional agendas to fulfill, just honest interactions. This one, intentional action by the teacher will help her/him to remember that s/he is teaching *students*, not subjects.

Following are potential topics/questions to post on chart paper for students to answer, many of which could develop from lunchroom conversations.

- What is your favorite genre to check out from our school library? (Two to three options listed, such as historical fiction, contemporary fiction, informational, fantasy.)

- What type of face should we carve on our class pumpkin? (Scary or silly?)

- Which version of Cinderella did you enjoy the most?

- Which activity do you like to do on a Saturday? (Play outside, read a book, watch TV, listen to music?)

- Which ice cream topping is your favorite? (Chocolate syrup, caramel, strawberry, plain?)

- Which movie should win an Academy Award? (List three of the most recent children's movies. Show a video clip of each so all children can participate, whether or not they've seen all the movies.)

Current Events as Graph Questions

As the English poet John Donne so insightfully wrote, "No man is an island," so, too, does this apply to children. They hear the news reports, see online posts, watch Youtube™ videos, listen to their parents' conversations, and talk to friends. Early-elementary students realize that the wide world around them impacts their daily lives. Teachers who tap into current events as subjects of classroom instruction convey to their students that they respect their world knowledge and that literacy empowers all citizens to think and act for the good of society. Possible topics or questions for use in early elementary classroom graphs include the following:

- Which playground equipment should our park district install in the new neighborhood park? (Swing set, climbing bars, slide . . . ?)

- What would you suggest our neighborhood do to improve the empty lot by our school? Have the students brainstorm several options and post them on the graph. Ideas could include: create a "pocket park" (small green area containing benches, small flower garden, and/or public art display), community garden, or walking path.

- Which candidate would you vote for mayor/president/park district board member/ . . . ? This should follow a brief discussion or display of each candidate's main platform and ideas for improvement as they relate to the students' lives.

- Which name for the new baby animal at our zoo do you like best? (Post the top three names the zoo is considering at that time.)

- In our letter to the newspaper about ____ issue, which topic should we focus on? (Brainstorm current concerns and post them on the graph.)

- Which of these picture books would you vote for to win the Caldecott Medal this year? (List three books written and illustrated in the United States during the current calendar year that the class has read together.) This award is announced during the American Library Association's midwinter meeting each January. Therefore, post this graph in the first two weeks of January and once the winner is announced, share the news with the class. Of course, celebrate the winner by reading the book aloud!

- What should our class make for our neighborhood shelter's Thanksgiving meal? (Design colorful placemats, assemble cutlery/napkin kits, create centerpieces, etc.)

HIT A HOMERUN WITH SPORTS-RELATED LITERACY MOMENTS

Early elementary students' popular culture includes sports: both as participants and as spectators. Teachers should capitalize on this motivating topic's appeal by creating literacy moments. Such opportunities include reading informational books about various seasonal sports or biographies of famous athletes, creating graphs related to local teams and favorite players, using scores and statistics for quantitative reasoning, and, ultimately, developing a community of learners by sharing in their enjoyment of this subject matter.

Vocabulary Development

Each sport has a unique vocabulary. During each sport's season, teachers could talk about their local team and create word walls containing that sport's specific terminology. For example, football is a prime fall sport, played on

Sunday afternoons and viewed throughout the nation. Therefore, teachers should post their local team's final score on the board on Monday morning and talk with their students about how their team performed. By how many points did they win (or lose)? If the teacher's childhood home team is a rival of the school's home team, s/he can have some competitive fun by posting each team's scores and comparing their progress throughout the season. During the Monday discussions, the teacher should intentionally interject football terminology, such as: touchdown, field goal, punt, wide receiver, defense, offense, etc. As the season progresses, each new term is added to the football word map.

Basketball is another great sport for interesting lingo and vocabulary activities. Most school playgrounds and gymnasiums have basketball hoops, so this could be easily integrated into physical activity. Regulation basketball hoops are likely too difficult for early-elementary students to use for shooting baskets. However, games such as dribbling drills are fun alternatives.

To play, the teacher gives a basketball to each student. On signal, the students stand in place and dribble the ball. Next, the teacher states, "I'm thinking of a term in basketball for when one player passes the ball to a teammate who jumps up and catches the ball then slam dunks it through the net. Is it . . . lay up? . . . free throw? . . . alley oop?" Students must stop dribbling when they hear the teacher state the correct term (in this case, "alley oop").

Baseball lingo is another prime area for expanding students' vocabulary. From balks to sliders to ribbies (runs batted in, or RBIs), springtime is the season for having fun with these unique baseball terms. Teachers could either read aloud a fun baseball-themed picture book or show a few highlights with announcers using one or two new baseball terms. They could follow this up by adding each new term to a baseball cutout and posting it on a board or word wall. Here are a few terms to get teachers started on their search for fun and unique baseball slang:

Bang-Bang Play: when a ball is thrown just in time to get a runner out (the sound of the ball hitting the glove right before the sound of the baserunner's foot hitting the base).
Can of Corn: a pop fly that is easy to catch.
Caught Looking: a batter strikes out without swinging the bat.
Cheese: fast ball.
Four Bagger; Dinger; Go Yard: all terms for hitting a homerun.
Paint the Corners: pitcher throws a pitch on the edge of home plate.
Table Setter: batter who gets a hit to set up the next batter for a homerun or base hit.
Walk Off: a batter makes a hit that scores the game-winning run.

Read-aloud Opportunities

When a local sports team reaches an important goal or a player achieves a special recognition, they become popular subjects of local news media. Teachers can intentionally scan their newspapers or digital media sources for brief, interesting articles about these current events. As part of the day's calendar time, the teacher should post the article's headline on the whiteboard and lead the beginning readers in a choral reading of it. Following a brief discussion, the teacher and students would celebrate their home team's achievements through the teacher's reading aloud of the article.

Take this literacy moment further by encouraging students to collect additional articles and bring them to class throughout the week. The student could be invited to read aloud the title or headline of his/her article and talk about why s/he brought it to share. Post the article on the board alongside the original article. Beginning readers will likely be motivated to share in this excitement and enjoy the opportunity to bring in their own articles. This is an authentic opportunity to create community among all learners in the classroom.

Additional Literacy Moments Related to Reading Sports Articles Aloud

- Player profiles: Encourage students to gather articles and biographies related to favorite players (both past and present) for the specific sport of that season. This could evolve into an informative classroom display, combining print media with books, posters, trading cards, etc.

- Creative writing: Is the local team not performing at a high level? Challenge students to make up their own fantasy headline and either write a short article (for older beginning readers) or illustrate the headline (for younger beginning readers). Display these artifacts alongside the collection of current articles or player profiles.

- Trading card mathematics: Share cards from digital media and/or trading card packages found at local stores. Talk about the statistics and create basic math problems about the statistics, applying currently studied numeracy skills. Challenge students to create their own math problems for their friends to solve, too.

OUR LIVES, OUR STORIES: DRAWING ON PERSONAL HISTORIES AS LITERACY MOMENTS

Human beings are natural storytellers; it is how we make sense of the world around us. We create a running narrative of our daily lives, personal experiences, and interactions with members of our communities. Furthermore, our stories reveal our ways of creating meaning while also developing our personal philosophies about life. From birth, young children are immersed in family narratives. Parents and caregivers talk to their infants in complete sentences, they make eye contact, use facial expressions, and convey meaning through voice inflections. This is a key component to young children's speech and language development (Flynn, 2016).

By the time young children enter Kindergarten, they have become expert storytellers. They describe family outings, weekend experiences, and more, to their friends and teachers. These personal histories inform each student's developing sense of cultural identity. They are very relevant and meaningful resources to use in the classroom for a variety of literacy moments, especially regarding their impact on speaking and listening development.

Teachers can tap into the rich resources of their students' parents, caregivers, and other community members by reaching out to them early in the school year. The initial contact should be to celebrate their children's accomplishments and share their successes. Teachers could then follow up with phone calls to the parents to ask a few questions about their student, such as how their child learns best. Once a relationship is formed, teachers and parents can have informal conversations about parents' hobbies, skills they'd like to share, etc. This will lend itself to having parents come in as guest speakers to tell a story about a favorite childhood memory.

Other community members should also become a resource for their stories, expertise, and ability to share any current social justice news or events. The teachers should keep a file to organize this information as a way to tap these resources for future classroom visits or project leadership (Cowhey, 2006).

Story Starters that Develop Speaking and Listening Skills

Create a list of story starters to use during unexpected moments when children are in transition from one activity to the next. By preparing this "tool box" of story ideas, teachers will be ready to capitalize on opportunities to share personal stories while elevating all students' cultures and nurturing their language development.

Here are a few story starters to put into teachers' tool boxes. After reading the starter aloud, teachers can model the process by providing their own response and then telling the students they can raise their hands when they're ready to add a personal response to the prompt.

- "I'll never forget when I learned how to . . ."
- "My favorite color is _____ because . . ."

- "My earliest memory is from when I was ___ years old. This is what I remember:"
- "My favorite place to sit and think is _____ because . . ."
- "If I were to go anywhere in the world, I'd want to go to _____ because . . ."
- "My favorite food that my [family member] makes is _____. It makes me feel _____ when they make it for me."
- "My most special family tradition is _____."
- "My favorite game to play outside is _____. This is how we play it:"
- "My family celebrates birthdays by [describe one activity]."
- "If we had no school for a week, I'd want to [describe activity]."

Children's Picture Books that Tell the Authors' Family Stories

A wonderful way to provide a mentor text of how storytellers convey their family history is to read aloud a variety of picture books that are based on the author's personal history. Such stories provide a foundation for promoting similar storytelling by the students in the classroom. They may stimulate questions for beginning readers to ask their parents about ("What happened on the day I was born?" "What games did you play when you were my age?").

After reading aloud from picture books about the authors' family history, teachers could tell a similar story about their ancestors. Next, they could encourage the students to record their parents, grandparents, aunts, uncles, and siblings, each telling a story about their favorite childhood memory. When students' parents send their families' recordings to the teacher, s/he could play the recording for the class to hear during a brief break in the day. This is a very effective way to foster community, celebrate one another's family history, and promote listening comprehension among beginning readers.

The following is a list of picture books based on the author's family history.

Ackerman, K. (1988). *Song and dance man.* New York: Scholastic.
Cooney, B. (1982). *Miss Rumphius.* New York: Trumpet.
dePaola, T. (1993). *Tom.* New York: Scholastic.
Houston, G. (1992). *My Great Aunt Arizona.* New York: HarperCollins.
Howard, E. F. (1991). *Aunt Flossie's hats (and crab cakes later).* Boston: Clarion Books.
Shelby, A. (1995). *Homeplace.* London: Orchard Books.
Williams, D. (1993). *Grandma Essie's covered wagon.* New York: Alfred A. Knopf.
Wyeth, S. D. (2013). *The granddaughter necklace.* New York: Arthur A. Levine Books.

Story Artifacts

Authors also create fictional accounts of families coming together to work through a significant event or situation. Beginning readers benefit from these stories, too, because they create a sense of camaraderie for students who may have had similar experiences. Such stories often include an artifact of significance to the author. After reading these stories, teachers can create an artifact box or suitcase and place tokens from the books inside. Each token is added to the collection following the reading of the book. The teacher should also add a personal artifact and briefly tell the story from his/her family experience.

Children can draw pictures of artifacts they have at home, such as stuffed animals that are significant to them, a special plate used for holidays, a favorite handmade blanket or scarf, etc. They would then tell their classmates the stories their artifact represents. Finally, the teacher should adhere the pictures to the box or suitcase to create a more permanent display. The following picture books tell stories about families' significant events or focus on special artifacts.

Croza, L. (2010). *I know here*. Toronto: Groundwood Books.
Flournoy, V. (1985). *The patchwork quilt*. New York: Dial.
Fox, M. (1989). *Wilfrid Gordon McDonald Partridge*. La Jolla, CA: Kane/Miller Books.
Hathorn, L. (1994). *Way home*. New York: Crown.
Hoffman, M. (2002). *The colour of home*. New York: Penguin Putnam Books.
Khan, R. (2010). *Big red lollipop*. New York: Viking.
Kurtz, J. (2005). *In the small, small night*. New York: Greenwillow Books.
Laínez, R. C., & Accardo, A. (2004). *Waiting for Papá/ Esperando a Papá*. Houston, TX: Piñata Books.
Martin Jr., B., & Archambault, J. (1987). *Knots on a counting rope*. New York: Trumpet.
Park, F. (2002). *Good-bye, 382 Shin Dang Dong*. Des Moines, IA: National Geographic Children's Books.
Perkins, L. R. (2007). *Pictures from our vacation*. New York: Greenwillow Books.
Sanna, F. (2016). *The journey*. London: Flying Eye Books.
Williams, V. (1982). *A chair for my mother*. New York: Scholastic.
Wong, J. (2002). *Apple pie 4th of July*. Orlando, FL: Harcourt.
Yolen, J. (1991). *All those secrets of the world*. Boston: Little, Brown.
Yolen, J. (1987). *Owl moon*. New York: Scholastic.

Autobiographical Picture Books

These books provide another excellent source of inspiration for encouraging beginning readers to think about their lives and select moments to turn into stories about themselves. After reading aloud from autobiographical picture books, teachers can tell a story from their own life that connects to the author's topic. Next, the teacher should lead the class in brainstorming a list of potential topics from the story that might relate to their students' experiences. The students would then select a topic from the list, turn to a neighbor, and share their own story as it relates to the topic.

Here are a few such picture books to set the foundation for thinking about our lives as sources for interesting stories to share.

Blos, J. (1994). *In the days before now: An autobiographical note by Margaret Wise Brown*. New York: Simon & Schuster.
Bridges, R. (1999). *Through my eyes*. New York: Scholastic.
Bryan, A. (2009). *Ashley Bryan: Words to my life's song*. New York: Atheneum.
Carle, E. (2011). *The artist who painted a blue horse*. New York: Philomel.
Crews, D. (1991). *Bigmama's*. New York: Trumpet.
dePaola, T. (1989). *The art lesson*. New York: G. P. Putnam's Sons.
Fanelli, S. (1995). *My map book*. New York: HarperCollins.
King, Jr., M. L. (2012). *I have a dream: Book & CD*. (Illustrated by Kadir Nelson). New York: Random House.
Polacco, P. (1991). *The keeping quilt*. New York: Simon & Schuster.
Rylant, C. (1982). *When I was young in the mountains*. New York: E. P. Dutton.
Say, A. (1993). *Grandfather's journey*. New York: Houghton Mifflin.
Stevenson, J. (1994). *Fun, no fun*. New York: Greenwillow Books.
Young, E. (2011). *The house Baba built: An artist's childhood in China*. Boston, MA: Little, Brown.

Quick Writes Based on Family Stories

While beginning readers develop their storytelling skills through these mentor texts, teachers can bridge oral and written language by facilitating literacy moments through the following brief written response activities.

Storytelling Notebooks

Teachers will best nurture their students' storytelling skills by developing a quick-write routine using storytelling notebooks. They should provide pocket-sized notebooks for each student and have them available each day for students to participate in spontaneous written responses based on books read aloud in class.

For example, following a reading of a book about family experiences, teachers could instruct their students to make a list in their notebooks of similar experiences they've had. They would then mark the items that are their favorites. This list will provide a resource for a future creative writing activity (adapted from Buckner, 2005).

Group Wordles™

After a book has been read aloud, teachers should distribute a 4 × 6 sheet of paper and instruct the students to write one word that they believe represents the most important idea in the book. Once the teacher has collected each word card, s/he will post them on the board and have students determine which words seem to be the most prevalent. Teacher and students will work together to arrange the words in a bar graph to visually organize them based on popularity.

Next, the teacher will describe and model how to rearrange the words to create a group Wordle™. They will use colorful markers to write the most popular words in the largest font, and the least popular words in smaller fonts. This could be done on sheets of construction paper and posted on a bulletin board with a copy of the book's cover page. The completed display will be a powerful word wall for beginning readers to refer to when writing future compositions related to the book's themes.

Word Maps

Teachers will instruct the students to draw a picture of themselves in the middle of a sheet of construction paper. Next, the children will draw lines (like spokes) away from their self-portraits and at the end of each spoke they will write a word that names something interesting about them. For example, after reading an autobiographical picture book, students would think about words for favorite traditions, memorable events, important people in their lives, etc. The final products could be displayed in the classroom and used as references for impromptu storytelling. When unexpected time becomes available, the teacher will randomly call on a student to pick a word from their self-portrait and tell the story it represents.

CONCLUDING THOUGHTS

Children's cultural experiences must be a driving force in the classroom. When teachers are consciously aware of creating and embracing a culturally responsive learning environment, they will intentionally seek opportunities to develop literacy moments rooted in their students' lived experiences. Throughout this chapter, various strategies and resources have been provided to facilitate this process. As teachers become more immersed in thinking about methods of connecting their students' cultures to the curriculum, they will naturally create authentic literacy moments each day.

REFERENCES

Ahmed, S. (2018). *Being the change: Lessons and strategies to teach social comprehension.* Portsmouth, NH: Heinemann.

Bartolomé, L. (1994). Beyond the methods fetish: Toward a humanizing pedagogy. *Harvard Review, 64,* 173–94.

Buckner, A. (2005). *Notebook know-how: Strategies for the writer's notebook.* Portland, ME: Stenhouse.

Compton-Lilly, C. (2003). *Reading families: The literate lives of urban children.* New York: Teachers College Press.

Cowhey, M. (2006). *Black ants and Buddhists: Thinking critically and teaching differently in the primary grades.* Portland, ME: Stenhouse Publishers.

Flynn, E. (2016). Language-rich early childhood classroom: Simple but powerful beginnings. *The Reading Teacher, 70,* 159–66.

Ladson-Billings, G. (1995). But that's just good teaching! The case for culturally relevant pedagogy. *Theory into Practice, 34*(3), 159–65.

Ladson-Billings, G. (1992). Culturally relevant teaching: The key to making multicultural education work. In C. A. Grant (Ed.) *Research and multicultural education* (pp. 106–21). London: Falmer Press.

Chapter Six

Integrating the Arts into Literacy Instruction

According to Sydney Gurewitz Clemens (2009), "Art has the role in education of helping children become more like themselves instead of more like everyone else" (par. 1). In teachers' efforts to provide beginning readers with literacy skills to enable their reading and writing development to progress *like everyone else*, they must be cognizant of the importance of infusing such instruction with opportunities for children to *become more like themselves* in the process. When teachers infuse literacy lessons with the arts—dance, music, visual art, and drama—they are fostering the development of creative expression and artistic appreciation in their young students, which they will likely carry with them and into their communities throughout their lives!

According to a survey conducted by the National Endowment for the Arts (2006), literacy and the arts have a reciprocal relationship in that those who choose to read for pleasure tend to also be more involved in the arts. Furthermore, "Americans who read books, visit museums, attend theater, and engage in other arts are more active in community life than those who do not" (p. 1). Put simply, the arts are integral to both society's quality of life and to the individual's development of creative expression. Art and education go hand in hand (Eisner, 1983). Early elementary classrooms must be safe spaces for their students' explorations of artistic responses to their world.

Most teachers do not see themselves as artists, therefore, they often become intimidated during discussions about integrating the arts into the curriculum. When teachers think about infusing the arts into literacy moments, however, they should think about intentionally incorporating creative expression, arts appreciation, and artistic development into their daily routines. In other words, integrating the arts into literacy moments does not necessarily entail teaching artistic techniques, music theory lessons, etc. Rather, teachers should see this as an opportunity to incorporate artistic elements throughout the day as a way to develop their beginning readers' literacy skills. Teachers should see their classroom environments and their lessons as canvases, ready for the teachers and their students to splash color and movement across the open domain!

TEACHERS AS ARTISTS: GETTING BEYOND THE CONCEPT OF ARTIST AS EXPERT

Before teachers embrace their self-perceptions as artists in their own right, they may need to take the time to nurture their innate creativity that has likely been buried over time. This will develop their capacity for artistic innovation. When we see ourselves as artistic beings, we seek out opportunities for creative expression. Furthermore, once teachers see themselves as creative, artistic individuals, they will emulate this mindset for their students. Following are a few examples of methods teachers can use to develop their creative mindsets.

- Go to the local library and browse their books on the subject of artistic expression (for those familiar with the Dewey Decimal cataloging system, go to the 150s section). Readers will find a plethora of books dedicated to rejuvenating and inspiring one's innate creativity. This is a very accessible way for all people to begin the process of exploring natural outlets of artistic expression in their daily lives.

- Get a copy of the classic book *The Artist's Way* (Cameron, 1992). It is available at most libraries or through an online bookstore that sells used books. The author requires the reader to not only reflect each day in a morning journal, she also obliges readers to indulge in weekly artist dates. Here, Cameron tells us, "you are receiving—opening yourself to insight, inspiration, guidance" (p. 18).

- Intentionally set aside time each week to take an excursion (i.e., an artist date) somewhere new: browse a vintage shop, stop in at the new music store in town, take a workshop at the community center to develop a new hobby, visit a local art gallery, stroll along a nature trail, try a new ethnic restaurant. The possibilities are endless. The key is to think about creating everyday opportunities for artistic moments.

- Turn daily routines and home environments into artistic expressions. For example, when setting the table for dinner one could think about arranging a quick centerpiece (cut flowers, seasonal artifacts, or trinkets on a cake stand . . .). The point here is to think about living spaces as possibilities for creative expression. Here are a few other ways to develop artistic living:

- What's on the coffee table? Clutter? Find a beautiful "coffee table book" to display, or adorn it with a decorative potpourri-filled bowl.

- Tea (or coffee) drinkers: drink from a vintage teacup and saucer instead of an old mug. Sip slowly without any distractions (work-related or otherwise).

- Reframe old photographs and rotate them throughout the year. Rearrange the photographs in groups throughout the house and incorporate memorable artifacts in and around the groupings.

- Play music while fulfilling daily tasks like cooking, folding laundry, washing dishes. With the modern conveniences of online radio platforms, music lovers can create playlists to hear a variety of music genres without interruptions. In the interest of increasing artistic experiences, one could intentionally select a musical genre that is unfamiliar: early jazz radio; Broadway tunes; classical; pop; R & B; etc.

- Celebrate the seasons with porch/patio/balcony container gardens. Whether living in a house or apartment, there is usually space for a container garden. This could be filled with decorative flowers, herbs, or vegetables. Once the growing season has passed, use the container to create seasonal arrangements. In the fall, this would entail pumpkins, gourds, or dried flowers. In the winter, the container could hold artfully arranged pinecones, evergreen branches, dried berries. Be creative!

- Reserve a space, such as the top of a book shelf, or a small table, to display seasonal books. Rather than simply stacking them with their spine facing out, think about displaying them with seasonal artifacts, some stacked, some upright with their covers facing out. This is especially eye-catching to do with cookbooks in the kitchen, if space is available.

• Go for walks and take pictures. The pictures will provide excellent sources of visual material for use at home or in the classroom. Additionally, as photographic skills evolve, one could experiment by taking pictures that zoom in on a detail, omit color, play around with the perspective or angle of the frame, etc. Take this further by sorting them into groups for later use, or finding poems that seem to convey similar feelings and match them to the pictures. Perhaps these will provide a creative writing prompt. There are many ways that photographs can be sources of inspiration!

- Visit museums! This is obvious, but so important. All museums—arts-based, historical, scientific, cultural, or thematic—are significant to the vitality of their communities and provide insightful information, as well as artistic experiences. They greatly enhance the quality of life for us all. Furthermore, beyond a visit to their exhibits, many offer lectures, events, and workshops. Finally, if possible, take the opportunity to become a member of a favorite museum. Members often receive additional magazines and members-only invitations to various events.

- Support community theatre. Modern society seems to attend movies or stay home to watch online entertainment and sports. It's important, however, to break this routine by attending live performances whenever possible. Many communities offer musicals and dramatic productions for all to enjoy.

- Keep a writer's notebook as a source of ideas and inspiration. This notebook's purpose will be to store one's dreams, goals, and aspirations as they relate to artistic living. To achieve the maximum benefit of this notebook, one should commit each day or weekend to writing a list of ideas related to a specific topic. Each new entry should start on a new, clean page with a heading or prompt for the daily list. Such prompts might begin with "List at least five . . ."
  - things you want to learn this year (i.e., a new language, craft, skill, or activity)
  - foods you want to learn to cook
  - hobbies you'd like to explore
  - artists' biographies you'd like to read
  - things that thrilled you when you were young
  - musicians you'd like to see in concert
  - presents you'd want for your birthday
  - reasons you love your career choice
  - poets you would enjoy reading
  - words to describe you

- Take time to create. There is an inner artist in each person, and this includes all artistic domains: visual arts, dramatic arts, music, crafts, and dance. Once we allow time for our artistic expression to manifest itself, we will make an effort to explore a variety of creative outlets. This could involve taking an art class, woodworking class, music lesson, dance lesson, etc. It should also involve intentionally making time to practice hobbies that nurture creativity. People set aside time for that which is important. Therefore, once people begin to think of themselves as artistic beings, they will look for opportunities and carve out space for the creation of their art. There are many more ways for teachers to nurture their creative souls—this list is only meant to lay a foundation upon which to build and grow in artistic living. The more teachers engage in these types of daily routines, the more they will embrace and explore new ways of integrating the arts into their classrooms.

DEVELOPING VISUAL LITERACY THROUGH PICTURE BOOK READ ALOUDS

There are a variety of ways to add artistic flair to a literacy moment. An especially effective method (that doesn't require the use of art supplies) is to nurture beginning readers' visual literacy during read-aloud time when sharing picture books. By definition, picture books are stories that rely on both the written and visual texts to convey the plot (Kiefer, 1995). This makes them the perfect tool to use as a visual literacy teachable moment.

In order to foster beginning readers' ability to interpret picture book illustrations, teachers will need to model this for them by discussing the illustrators' uses of the visual elements: color, line, shape, texture, and composition. This means pausing during the read aloud and demonstrating to the students how the illustrator conveyed meaning through any of the elements that seem appropriate to that particular illustration at that particular point in the book. Teachers should ask, "How does the visual art communicate the story's plot, mood, theme?" Once teachers have immersed their students in such investigative viewing of the pictures, they should encourage their students' ability to look closely by asking a few guiding questions. This will facilitate their students' development of visual literacy by encouraging them to "read" not only the words on the page, but also the picture book illustrations.

See Table 6.1 for a chart of visual elements' definitions (Cornett, 2015, p. 236) and sample questions that would foster beginning readers' visual literacy during a picture-book read aloud.

VISUAL ART ACTIVITIES TO SUPPORT FOUNDATIONAL READING SKILLS

With the easy access of famous artists' works on the internet, classroom teachers have the ability to quickly integrate seminal art pieces into literacy

Table 6.1. Developing Visual Literacy through Picture Book Illustrations

Visual Element	Definition and Usage	Sample Questions to Facilitate Visual Literacy
Color	Hues (color names) that are created by wavelengths of light. Often, the illustrator will convey feelings through color choices, such as: Red = anger, intense emotion, passion Orange = warmth Yellow = bright, excited, happy, light Green = envy, pride, or earthy, cool Blue = sadness, cool Purple = royalty	How do you feel when you look at this picture? How did the illustrator use color to make you feel this way?
Line	A series of dots drawn next to each other that creates a path. Horizontal and vertical lines typically represent stability, while diagonal lines convey anxiety or action. Smooth curves convey relaxation. Thick lines convey strength while thin lines suggest frailty.	Why do you suppose the illustrator has all the characters moving in a straight line across the page? Would you go into this forest? How do the lines of the trees and branches support your answer?
Shape	Lines that enclose a space—geometric or rounded. Round shapes convey organic/natural life. Geometric shapes may convey tension.	Why do you suppose you're afraid/not afraid of this character? How did the illustrator draw the character to make you feel this way?
Texture	The illustrator's use of line, color, and shape to portray how an object would feel to touch it.	How does the illustrator convey the surface of this tree (for example)?
Composition	The arrangement of all elements on the page to create the overall picture.	Do you feel anxious when you look at this picture? How did the illustrator make you feel this way? Why do you suppose the illustrator placed the characters in this space and the rest of the setting over here?

moments throughout the school year. When teachers have an artistic mindset, they are more likely to take advantage of the internet's plethora of art images displayed by museums around the world. Here are several literacy moments that stem from viewing visual art.

Word Study Skills Development: "I Spy"

Post the image of a famous scene, still life, or collage and play "I Spy" with a twist! Instead of telling students the name of the object they need to locate, have them practice a recently acquired word recognition skill by stating a clue about the object they need to locate in the picture. For example, when looking at Doris Lee's *Thanksgiving* (ca. 1935), say, "I spy with my little eye something that starts with the /pl/ blend." (Answer = plates)

More advanced challenges would be to find two items that end in the same rime, or word family, such as: dog/log; room/broom; cat/hat, etc. Teachers should project the image onto their whiteboard so that they can circle the objects as students name them, as well as write the words and underline the phonics/word study rule as they apply to the clue. This makes the verbal answers become visual reference points.

A wonderful picture book collection of famous works of art that encourages readers to find objects that start with each letter of the alphabet is *I Spy: An Alphabet in Art*, devised and selected by Lucy Micklethwait (1992). This book would be an effective way to facilitate beginning readers' understanding of how to play the game before progressing into more difficult word patterns to search. Additional paintings that are conducive to playing "I Spy" include, but certainly are not limited to, the following:

Sunday Afternoon on the Island of La Grande Jatte by Georges Seurat (ca. 1884)
Quilting Bee at Arles by Faith Ringgold (1991)
The Mechanization of the Country by Diego Rivera (1926)
The Bedroom at Arles by Vincent Van Gogh (1888)
The Bus by Frida Kahlo (1929)
Paris Street; Rainy Day by Gustave Caillebotte (1877)
Children's Games by Pieter Bruegel (1560)
The Dancing Couple by Jan Steen (1663)

Vocabulary Development: Picture Labels

Large reproductions of renowned paintings are excellent materials for developing both art appreciation and vocabulary. Teachers can post the print on a bulletin board at the beginning of the month and discuss the title and artist with the students to acquaint them with the new picture. Next, they should have students name several items they see in the picture. As they are named, the teacher prints the word on cardstock and adheres it near the object in the print. As the word is spelled, the teacher will slowly sound it out, then have the students read it aloud, and discuss it further by noting any word patterns similar to those already learned.

As the month progresses, the teacher will continue to solicit additional words for items in the art print. Once this is exhausted, the teacher should ask for words to describe how this picture makes them feel. These words will be posted around the perimeter of the print. Additional word and description categories include: adjectives, adverbs, verbs, synonyms, or antonyms. The categories will change as the types of artwork change over the course of the year. Throughout the month, the teacher should add definitions and sentences to the bulletin board, as appropriate and needed by the students. They should also encourage the students to use the words in daily oral and written language activities, as well as independent compositions.

Fun with Words

After viewing and discussing a work of art, teachers could develop vocabulary and word study by writing one word to describe something in the picture. Then, they would post a question as a word challenge to their students. For example, if a person in a painting is portrayed in motion, the teacher would post a word to name this motion. Then s/he would post the question: "How many words can you think of to describe his/her movement?" The challenge is for students to write a list of words within a time limit. When time is up, the children turn to their neighbors and share their word lists. They could add new words to their lists, too. Finally, the whole class would share their words to make a "community word list" which will be posted, along with the question, next to the picture.

Additional vocabulary-building questions include:

- This picture has a lot of [color] in it. How many words can you think of that state a feeling this color conveys? List them in your notebook. [For inspiration, teachers should read aloud several poems from Mary O'Neill's (1961) *Hailstones and Halibut Bones: Adventures in Color*.]

- If you could touch the objects in this picture, how would they feel? In your writer's notebook, list words to describe the textures you would feel.

- What mood has the artist created here? List all the words you can think of to describe the mood of this picture.

Art and Text

There are a variety of children's books that cleverly connect famous works of art with thematic vocabulary and narrative texts. Some excellent sources include the following:

- Bob Raczka has edited several books that combine basic reading skills with famous paintings in his series "Bob Raczka's Art Adventures." Some interesting titles include: *Art Is* (2003); *No One Saw: Ordinary Things through the Eyes of an Artist* (2009); *More Than Meets the Eye: Seeing Art with all Five Senses* (2003); *3-D ABC: A Sculptural Alphabet* (2006); *Artful Reading* (2009); *Name That Style: All About Isms in Art* (2009); and *Speaking of Art: Colorful Quotes by Famous Painters* (2009).

- In addition to her "I Spy" book, Lucy Micklethwait has published several series of books that encourage looking closely at famous works of art, including: *A Child's Book of Art: Great Pictures—First Words* (1993); *A Child's Book of Play in Art* (1996); *Children: A First Art Book* (2008); *I Spy Shapes in Art* (2004); *I Spy Colors in Art* (2007).

Concrete Poems

Teachers can merge vocabulary development with artistic expression by sharing samples of concrete poems with their students and then having them create their own. Concrete poems are collections of words shaped into the subject of the poem. So, a poem about an ice cream cone would have the words conveying this subject arranged in the shape of an ice cream cone. This is a creative way to enhance beginning readers' vocabulary development as they must first brainstorm various words that would convey the essence of their subject. Teachers could use this poetic form to reinforce new vocabulary from their science and social studies classes, too. Several poets have published collections of concrete poems, including:

Janeczko, P. (2001). *A poke in the I: A collection of concrete poems.* Somerville, MA: Candlewick Press.
Janeczko, P. (2005). *A kick in the head: An everyday guide to poetic forms.* Somerville, MA: Candlewick Press.
Raczka, B. (2016). *Wet cement: A mix of concrete poems.* New York: Roaring Brook Press.
Roemer, H. (2004). *Come to my party: And other shape poems.* New York: Henry Holt.

Chapter Six

LITERACY MOMENTS VIA ART ACTIVITIES

Children are creative beings. So, too, are adults! Teachers understand that children learn best when they're given the opportunity to explore ideas and participate in hands-on experiences. Beginning readers thrive when they are involved in authentic activities that nurture creative expression. Therefore, the following activities are provided to give early-elementary teachers inspiration for facilitating their students' creativity through literacy moments.

Provide Artistic "How-To" Books Written for Beginning Readers

Informational picture books that describe basic art activities for beginning readers are excellent sources for reading with a purpose. In this case, reading serves the purpose of helping people to enjoy their hobbies. By placing several such books in a learning station, along with crayons, paper, and basic art supplies, teachers will provide their students with authentic reading practice while promoting creative expression. Teachers can access these books in the children's department of their local library. Informational craft books are found in the Dewey Catalog Section of 745.5.

In the learning station, children select a project from the book, read the step-by-step directions, and create the project using the station's supplies. Through this station, beginning readers apply their word recognition skills to real-world reading. Here are a few "how-to" books that are written for beginning readers.

- Usborne Book Publishers has a series called "Usborne Playtime" by Ray Gibson. Each book in the series provides step-by-step instructions, in both words and pictures, to guide beginning readers in drawing a variety of objects, from people to animals to everyday items. The titles in this series include: *I Can Crayon* (1997), *I Can Draw Animals* (1998), *I Can Draw People* (2000), and *What Shall I Draw?* (1995).

- Ed Emberley has created a plethora of "how to draw" books for many decades. These classic informational books are appropriate to include in this learning station; however, they do not include written text. Therefore, they don't provide practice in reading basic sentence structures and matching the words to the pictures.

Illustrated Language Experience Stories

As described in Chapter 4, language experiences stem from authentic activities shared by all students together. Therefore, after the class returns from a

Figure 6.1. Illustrated language experience approach for a trip to the apple orchard.
Photo credit: J. Witter-Easley

field trip or guest speaker's presentation, they could dictate the events to the teacher as s/he writes them on large chart paper. Once the children's dictation is concluded, the teacher will cut apart each sentence and adhere it to a large blank piece of paper. Next, pair up the students to work together in creating an illustration on their paper that accurately represents the sentence that was adhered to their page. Finally, collate each page in sequential order of events and create a class book that retells the story of their recent activity. See Figure 6.1 for an example.

Create Illustrations and Text for Wordless Picture Books

This activity is similar to the illustrated language experience stories described above. In this activity, after the teacher shares a wordless book with the class, s/he should go back to the beginning and tell the class that they will dictate the story in their own words. As students provide sentences for each illustration, with the teacher guiding their process so that the story progresses with the author's plot, the teacher writes their sentences on chart paper. Next, the teacher cuts each sentence apart, adheres it to a blank sheet of paper, and has pairs of students collaborate to create an illustration to go with their part of

Figure 6.2. Illustrated wordless picture book for *The Snowman* by Raymond Briggs (1978).
Photo credit: J. Witter-Easley

the story. Finally, the teacher collates the pages in order and reads the students' version of the book aloud to the class. See Figure 6.2 for an example using Raymond Briggs' (1978) *The Snowman*.

Sketchbooks and Read Alouds

At the beginning of each month, teachers could provide each student with a sketchbook. This is made by folding five 9 × 12 white sheets of construction paper in half with one colored sheet of paper at the bottom of the stack and stapling the stack together along the fold, or spine, of the booklet. Students decorate the cover of the book and write the month at the top.

During the month, after various picture books are read aloud, the students will write the book's author and title on the next blank page and draw an illustration that conveys the plot or theme of the book. By the end of each month, the children will have created a personal log book of all the read alouds they enjoyed in school. This is an excellent way to provide children and their families with information about favorite books. It will be a handy reference for family trips to the library, or for birthday and holiday wish lists!

Quick Draw Activities

Teachers can merge their word walls with creative expression through quick draws. First, they should select one vocabulary word from a thematic word collection (words based on key terms from a content-area class such as science, social studies, math, etc.). They will then write the word on the whiteboard and tell students to draw a picture that shows the meaning of the word. After a time limit, students hold up their pictures while also viewing their peers' illustrations. Discuss several pictures and facilitate the students' understanding of the vocabulary word.

INTEGRATING MUSIC AND MOVEMENT INTO LITERACY MOMENTS

Because music is naturally integrated into our lives every day, from radio programs to online platforms to television shows to advertisements to humming or whistling while we work, it is fitting to intentionally integrate it into the classroom learning environment, too. According to Cornett (2015), music drives creativity and learning, increases our ability to pay attention and remember information, promotes positive thinking, affirms cultural identity, and encourages collegiality (pp. 466–69). Moreover, music enhances beginning readers' literacy development through each of these benefits. To foster a musical environment, try some of the following:

- *Play music in the background*—Whenever students are required to take a few minutes to discuss a topic with a partner or small group, play soft instrumentals in the background, such as classical, jazz, new age, or nature sounds. By immersing students in music during their discussions or seatwork time, teachers are exposing them to new musical genres while providing a soothing learning environment.

- *Use music for transition time*—Throughout the day, students complete seatwork, write in their notebooks, participate in small-group projects, etc. When they finish their work and turn it in, teachers could facilitate this transitional time by leading the class in singing a quick song. This technique not only encourages singing, it also provides a time frame for the transition so that time on task is maximized. Teachers could make up a song to a common tune, or simply sing a folksong. When the teacher begins the song, the students are signaled that it's time to wrap up their independent work time. As they join in to sing along, they turn in their work and return to their seats by the end of the song.

> **TEXTBOX 6.1. SAMPLE "TRANSITION SONG"**
>
> **Seatwork Song (Tune: London Bridge)**
> It's time to finish up our work,
> Up our work,
> Up our work.
> It's time to finish up our work,
> So please stop.
>
> Remember to write your name at the top,
> Name at the top,
> Name at the top.
> Remember to write your name at the top,
> And turn it in!

At the beginning of the year, the teacher would have the lyrics posted on chart paper and teach the students to read the words, underlining common sight words first, then circling new vocabulary terms, then tracking the text as they lead the class in a choral reading of the words. Finally, the teacher tracks the text again, this time leading the students in reading the words to the tune of the folksong (see sample in Textbox 6.1).

- *Rhythmic Clapping*—Another impactful transition method, this time for getting students' attention at the beginning of a new lesson, is to engage them in rhythmic clapping. Rather than raising their voices above the hum of students, teachers should simply clap, snap, tap, or slap their hands in a rhythmic pattern, repeating it until all the students have learned the pattern and successfully joined in. For example, as the students are putting away supplies and chatting, the teacher moves to the front of the room and claps his/her hands twice, snaps fingers once, and taps his/her shoulders twice, then repeats the pattern. Without saying a word, the students look up and watch carefully, joining in as they learn the pattern. Once they've all joined in, they are attentive and ready to participate in the next activity.

  This activity is also effective for connecting new word patterns/rimes, too. Simply assign a hand movement to each letter of a new rime. So, for the rime /-at/, hands would clap for /a/ and slap knees for /t/. Then as the words are read aloud to reinforce this rime, teacher and students clap hands and slap knees at the appropriate time for each word.

- *Take a Dance Break*—A wide variety of children's music is available to use as dance breaks. The teacher could play a fun song and lead the students in creative movement activities to shake out their wiggles. Early elementary students benefit greatly from these breaks because they provide time to allow for creative movement as well as a positive way to channel pent up energy and refocus their attention on the next lesson or activity.

When playing a song with a repeated chorus or refrain, the teacher can promote beginning reading skills by printing the chorus on chart paper. As the chorus is sung, the teacher tracks the print and has the class read/sing along, pausing their dancing while doing so. As the next verse begins, the dancing resumes. Following are excellent sources of music for dance breaks.

- *Disney's For Our Children: To Benefit the Pediatric AIDS Foundation* (1990)—This CD is a collection of children's songs sung by famous musicians. A personal favorite for silly dancing is Little Richard's version of "The Itsy Bitsy Spider"!

- *Disney's For Our Children Too: To Benefit the Pediatric AIDS Foundation* (1996)—Another excellent compilation of children's songs by renowned artists.

- Jim Gill—His original songs with a variety of rhythms, about both meaningful and nonsense topics, are always a big hit with early elementary students. He has produced many CDs over the last twenty years. Some of his more popular CDs are *Jim Gill Makes It Noisy in Boise, Idaho* (1995); *Jim Gill Sings the Do Re Mi on His Toe, Leg, Knee* (1999); *Jim Gill's Irrational Anthem* (2001); and *Jim Gill Sings the Sneezing Song and Other Contagious Tunes: 20th Anniversary Edition* (2013).

- Movie Soundtracks—Many children's movies and family musicals contain several movement-inspiring songs. Classic favorites include: *Mary Poppins Original Soundtrack* (1964); *Chitty Chitty Bang Bang Original Soundtrack* (1968); *The Sound of Music* (1965); *Beauty and the Beast Original Motion Picture Soundtrack* (1991); *The Little Mermaid Original Motion Picture Soundtrack* (1989); *The Music Man* (1962); *Singing in the Rain* (1952); *Despicable Me* (2010); *Hamilton* (2015); and many, many more! This is a wonderful way to introduce beginning readers to both classic and modern musicals.

- Online dance videos are a great source of instant literacy moments using dance and lyrics to apply newly learned word recognition skills through creative movement. GoNoodle.com is an excellent supplier of dance videos specifically for classroom use.

- Integrate hip-hop as a poetic form and incorporate movement when reading it aloud. An award-winning collection of poems written in the genre of hip-hop is *Hip-Hop Speaks to Children: A Celebration of Poetry with a Beat* (edited by Nikki Giovanni, 2008). This collection of poetry contains works by highly regarded children's and adult's poets. It also includes an audio CD with thirty of the poems read aloud by the original poets. This is an integral resource for all classrooms.

- Get to know children's musicians. Aside from Jim Gill (mentioned earlier), many excellent musicians create music for young audiences. They incorporate movement and literacy skills into their songs, in addition to melodic play. Following are some well-known children's musicians (both modern and classic) who provide worthwhile opportunities for integrating music into literacy moments:
  - Laurie Berkner
  - Tom Chapin
  - The Deedle Deedle Dees
  - Woody Guthrie
  - Ella Jenkins
  - Lucky Diaz and the Family Jam Band
  - The Not-Its
  - Hap Palmer
  - Raffi
  - Justin Roberts
  - They Might Be Giants (yes, the same alternative '80s band has now created an award-winning children's CD)

• *Song Lyrics to Support Content Areas*—Teachers can integrate songs into their content areas by substituting folksong lyrics with content from a scientific unit of study or about a famous person from history, for example. When learning about new content, the teacher will introduce the song and teach the students the lyrics (written on chart paper). Next, highlight key vocabulary from the unit, as well as words that follow phonics rules or morphemic patterns that have been learned during English Language Arts class. Through this activity, students are applying both content area knowledge and foundational reading skills to singing the new song. See Figure 6.3 for an example.

PICTURE BOOKS FEATURING MUSIC AND SONGS

Picture books based on folksongs provide authentic word recognition opportunities. As children sing to the familiar song lyrics, they are matching them to their

Figure 6.3. Photograph of student circling sight words on chart containing lyrics to song about Andrew Carnegie (tune: *Three Blind Mice*)

Photo credit: J. Witter-Easley

printed words on the page. Teachers can project the book onto a whiteboard so that all students can sing and follow along with the words on the book's pages.

It's best to sing the entire song while the teacher holds up the picture book for all to see the words and illustrations. Then, the teacher should go back to the beginning and project the book onto the whiteboard, singing the lyrics and underlining the words as they are sung. The teacher could highlight (draw a box around) a word that uses a recently learned phonics rule or word pattern.

Several websites provide lists of illustrated folksongs in picture book format. Teachers will want to share folksongs from a wide variety of cultures, including all of the cultural backgrounds represented in their classrooms. Online lists are typically well-maintained and provide up-to-date information on both classic folk songs and modern songs from all cultures. One such website is from the Center for Lifelong Music Making (lifelongmusicmaking.org/songbooks.html). This website also provides details about effective ways to teach children the lyrics to folksongs.

CONCLUDING THOUGHTS

The arts are integral to our quality of life and provide a pathway for us to develop our creative instincts and bring beauty into the world. Teachers of beginning readers can quickly integrate artistic moments into their students' literacy development. Doing so will not only enhance their reading and writing skills, it will also immerse them in an artistic mindset, thereby allowing them to nurture their own creativity throughout the day, beyond art or music class time. The ideas contained in this chapter provide a starting point for teachers to use as a foundation for their own development in integrating creative expression into their students' literacy moments.

REFERENCES

Cameron, J. (1992). *The artist's way: A spiritual path to higher creativity*. New York: Penguin Putnam, Inc.
Clemens, S. G. (2009). Art in the classroom: Making every day special. Retrieved from http://webshare.northseattle.edu/fam180/topics/art/Art%20in%20the%20 Classroom.htm.
Cornett, C. (2015). *Creating meaning through literature and the arts: Arts integration for classroom teachers* (5th ed.). Boston, MA: Pearson.
Eisner, E. (1983). *Beyond creating*. Los Angeles: Getty Center for Education in Art.
Kiefer, B. (1995). *The potential of picture books: From visual literacy to aesthetic understanding*. Englewood Cliffs, NJ: Prentice Hall.
National Endowment for the Arts. (2006). *The arts and civic engagement: Involved in arts, involved in life*. Washington, DC: National Endowment for the Arts.

CHILDREN'S BOOKS CITED

Briggs, R. (1978). *The snowman*. New York: Random House.
Gibson, R. (1995). *What shall I draw?* London: Usborne Books.
Gibson, R. (1997). *I can crayon*. London: Usborne Books.
Gibson, R. (1998). *I can draw animals*. London: Usborne Books.
Gibson, R. (2000). *I can draw people*. London: Usborne Books.

Giovanni, N. (Ed.) (2008). *Hip-hop speaks to children: A celebration of poetry with a beat*. Naperville, IL: Sourcebooks, Inc.
Micklethwait, L. (1992). *I spy: An alphabet in art*. New York: HarperCollins.
Micklethwait, L. (1993). *A child's book of art: Great pictures—first words*. New York: DK Publishing.
Micklethwait, L. (1996). *A child's book of play in art*. New York: DK Publishing.
Micklethwait, L. (2004). *I spy shapes in art*. New York: Greenwillow Books.
Micklethwait, L. (2007). *I spy colors in art*. New York: Greenwillow Books.
Micklethwait, L. (2008). *Children: A first art book*. London: Frances Lincoln Children's Books.
O'Neill, M. (1961). *Hailstones and halibut bones: Adventures in color*. New York: Doubleday & Doubleday, Inc.
Raczka, B. (2003). *Art is*. Minneapolis, MN: Millbrook Press.
Raczka, B. (2003). *More than meets the eye: Seeing art with all five senses*. Minneapolis, MN: Millbrook Press.
Raczka, B. (2006). *3-D ABC: A sculptural alphabet*. Minneapolis, MN: Millbrook Press.
Raczka, B. (2009). *Artful reading*. Minneapolis, MN: Millbrook Press.
Raczka, B. (2009). *Name that style: All about isms in art*. Minneapolis, MN: Millbrook Press.
Raczka, B. (2009). *No one saw: Ordinary things through the eyes of an artist*. Minneapolis, MN: Millbrook Press.
Raczka, B. (2009). *Speaking of art: Colorful quotes by famous painters*. Minneapolis, MN: Millbrook Press.

Part 3

Literacy Moments for Developing Comprehension Processes— An Introduction

Teachers of beginning readers often face a dilemma: they feel compelled to focus their literacy instructional time on decoding processes more so than on comprehension processes. As beginning readers move toward middle- and upper-elementary grades, however, they need to have mastered their word recognition skills and developed their abilities to think critically about text. In other words, "what matters in reading instruction matters because ultimately it affects whether the student develops into a reader who can comprehend what is in text" (Pressley, 2000, p. 545).

In Part 3, readers will find chapters devoted to creating literacy moments during each phase of the reading process: pre-reading, during reading, and post-reading. Chapter 7 focuses on pre-reading, ensuring that teachers will attend to teaching their young readers how to access their schema as it relates to the book they're about to read, and how to set a purpose for reading. The purposes will typically entail guiding students in setting one of two reading *stances*: efferent for informational text, and aesthetic for fiction.

Chapter 8 emphasizes creating literacy moments during the reading of any text. Here, teachers intentionally model active thinking processes as they lead the class in reading a common book, article, or text. A key element for teachers to implement during reading is to ask questions that foster higher levels of comprehension. This is a mindset shift from saving questions until the end of the text. Instead, teachers engage their beginning readers in the process of constructing meaning while they are reading, modeling thinking processes through think alouds, and asking questions at each level of comprehension: literal, inferential, and evaluative.

While reading the text, teachers will serve their students well by creating organizational charts that facilitate students' comprehension by filling in key information as they read. Ultimately, teachers will create these literacy moments that serve to heighten their students' comprehension into critical thinking levels, while also modeling the process of monitoring their thinking to ensure they understand the text and can implement strategies to repair any moments when comprehension may break down.

Finally, in Chapter 9, readers explore brief, authentic responses to text after it has been read. Here, teachers are challenged to create literacy moments that allow the time and space for authentic, meaningful responses to the texts, similar to those conducted by readers in the real world. The post-reading responses involve small-group discussions and written responses. The overall goal is to foster meaningful interactions between the students, teacher, and text that engage the group in critical thinking and reflection.

Throughout these three chapters, readers will become immersed in the mindset that comprehension is a process, not a product. It emerges as beginning readers encounter a book's cover, develops throughout their active thinking as they read, and evolves into new ways of knowing long after they close the book. When teachers intentionally create literacy moments that engage beginning readers in thinking throughout each phase of their reading journey, they will set them up for success as they enter their later years of schooling, and become members of society's literacy club (Smith, 1988).

REFERENCES

Pressley, M. (2000). What should comprehension instruction be the instruction of? (pp. 545–61). In M. Kamil, P. Mosenthal, P. D. Pearson, & R. Barr (Eds.) *Handbook of reading research: Volume III*. Mahwah, NJ: Lawrence Erlbaum Associates.

Smith, F. (1988). *Joining the literacy club: Further essays into education*. Portsmouth, NH: Heinemann.

Chapter Seven

Pre-Reading Literacy Moments That Foster Comprehension

How do good readers approach a new text (trade book, textbook, article, poem, etc.) to read? In what ways do good readers access their schema prior to reading a text? These are two critical questions for teachers to ask themselves because their answers will greatly inform the methods they use to foster comprehension before engaging their beginning readers in a new book or article. According to Anderson (1994), "comprehension is a matter of activating or constructing a schema that provides a coherent explanation of objects and events mentioned in a discourse" (p. 473). Therefore, teachers of beginning readers need to both activate their students' schema AND teach their students how to accurately access their own schemata.

Accessing schema before reading a text will provide readers with a personal connection to the book before they begin to read it (Harvey & Goudvis, 2007). When readers make a personal connection, their attention to the book's content is heightened, thereby increasing their level of comprehension. Furthermore, when the teacher provides opportunities for students to make these connections prior to reading the book, s/he is modeling for the beginning readers one of the thought processes made by effective readers: they anticipate content and make connections to determine how to approach the reading of the text (Gallagher, 2004).

When teachers make time for thinking prior to reading a text, they ensure that their students will anticipate content, set a purpose for reading, think critically while reading, and reflect metacognitively after reading. It is important, therefore, for teachers to thoughtfully consider the types of thinking in which to engage their readers. In other words, teachers need to consider the stance their beginning readers must take prior to reading the text in order to maximize their comprehension.

According to Rosenblatt (1995), readers' minds must be active as they construct meaning while reading the words on the page. This construction is a cognitive transaction that occurs between the reader, the text, and the author. Before they read any text, effective readers take on a specific stance, or perspective, that allows them to anticipate content and focus on textual information that supports their stance. When readers focus their thoughts on anticipating and comprehending factual information, they take on an efferent stance (p. 32). Alternatively, when readers focus on the literary art of the text and make connections to personal experiences, they take on an aesthetic stance (p. 31).

Teachers need to facilitate their beginning readers' abilities to anticipate content based on each of these stances because each stance has merit and serves a purpose. When teachers have identified the purpose for having students read any given text, they must then plan pre-reading activities designed to both access the appropriate schemata as well as signify the type of thinking required of the reader. Following are literacy moments designed to foster both efferent and aesthetic thinking as pre-reading activities.

PRE-READING LITERACY MOMENTS THAT EMPHASIZE AN EFFERENT STANCE

Quick Think: What Do You Know?

Prior to reading an informational book about a topic, introduce the book's title and ask the students to turn to a friend and tell him/her two or three things they know about the topic. After each friend has shared their ideas, tell the pairs to choose one of their facts to share with the class. The teacher will list the ideas on the board as each pair is called upon. There will likely be repeated ideas, so the list won't be too long. The teacher will reread each item on the list, encouraging the beginning readers to chorally read along, too. Next, the class will decide on which facts they believe will be described in the book—circle those facts on the list.

As the teacher reads the book aloud, the students will raise their hands when they hear one of their facts read aloud. They will put their thumbs up when they hear a new fact that was not on the list. The teacher will create a list with the new information so that the class can compare/contrast the information contained in the book with the ideas they already knew. If students contributed ideas that contained misinformation, discuss why this is so—or use the information in the book to guide them in drawing this conclusion.

Wordy Wonders

The teacher will read aloud the book title, showing the cover of the book to the class. S/He will list up to ten key words on the board, including several words that imply similar content but are NOT included in the actual text. Next, s/he will engage the students in reading the words aloud while tracking each word slowly, modeling how to read word parts or letter clusters, such as onsets and rimes (instead of individual letter sounds). The teacher will then talk about the words, emphasizing those which may be new vocabulary terms. Finally, the teacher challenges the students to copy down on an index card any words they believe will NOT be included in the upcoming text.

While reading the text aloud, the students will listen for these key words and draw a line through any words on their index card that is included in the book. By the end of the reading, the students can share the words they have left on their cards and talk about how they might convince the author to meaningfully include the unused words in the book.

True or False?

Teachers could make a class set of true/false response cards on index cards with "true" typed in bold font on one side and "false" on the other. The teacher will prepare several statements about important information contained in the book. After reading aloud the title and discussing the cover of the book, the teacher will instruct the students to hold up their card to indicate whether they believe the statement is true or false. As the teacher reads the prepared statements, s/he will allow some time for discussion, especially when conflicting opinions arise. If varying responses cannot be resolved, they'll have to read to learn the answer. The teacher will read a difficult statement last, one which will likely cause students to be unsure in their responses. This will set a purpose: "Let's read to find out whether this is true or false . . ."

Text Structure Prompts

Informational books are typically organized into a text structure that frames the way information is presented to the readers. For example, when the goal is to compare and contrast two concepts, the text typically alternates paragraphs or pages containing similar items first and differences next. If the information is described, authors tend to arrange information into types of characteristics: physical, relational, etc. Teachers can use this information to frame a quick pre-reading activity via graphic organizers. When teachers create these organizers on chart paper, they can post them around the room to use as content-area word walls.

For example, if the information is conveyed as comparing and contrasting two concepts, the teacher should draw a Venn Diagram on the board and write the name of each concept, one per circle in the diagram. Next, the teacher will lead the students in brainstorming a few ideas that they already know about each concept. Finally, the teacher sets the purpose for reading: to add new information about each concept, paying close attention to content that is similar to both (for the overlapping areas of the circles). Students will listen carefully and raise their hand when they hear about information that should be added to the diagram while the teacher reads aloud. Additional organizers for specific text structures include:

Time Line or Numerical Chart

This chart is for information contained in sequential order: start off with the first step and instruct students to read or listen to then add the next steps in the process sequentially in the flow chart. They will look for signal words: first, next, then, last; initially . . . ; finally.

Flow Chart

This is for information conveyed through cause and effect. These could be arranged horizontally, with the cause on the left and the arrow pointing to the effect on the right. Teachers should let children in on the secret to determining whether a book is arranged in cause-effect fashion; they will need to look for key words such as: if, then; as a result . . . ; since . . . ; because.

Super Stars

Teachers can use this format for content that conveys definitions of new concepts. Draw a large five-pointed star on the board. In the top point, write a key word or concept and generate ideas from the students regarding its meaning. As the book is read aloud, students listen for accuracy in their predicted definition. They also listen for and identify information to put around the word within the four remaining points in the star: examples of the concept, new information about the concept, characteristics of the concept, questions about the concept. After reading the book, discuss new information and questions generated.

Book Jacket Questions

Before reading aloud an informational book, the teacher should hold up the book and read the title to the class. Next, the teacher will walk around the room, instructing students to think about questions that come to mind upon scanning the images or words on the book jacket. Here, the students generate the questions—this requires critical thinking about the book and fosters creative inquiry (Ostroff, 2016). The teacher will then place the book jacket on the whiteboard ledge and have students share their questions. The teacher will write the questions on the board around the book jacket in dialog bubbles. At this point, the teacher may need to guide students to ask questions about images that allude to key concepts covered in the book. These questions will set a purpose for reading. As the teacher reads aloud, s/he will pause to allow students opportunities to contribute answers to their questions. The teacher will write the answers by the questions, leading the students in chorally reading the sentences aloud as they are written.

PRE-READING LITERACY MOMENTS THAT EMPHASIZE AN AESTHETIC STANCE

Pop Up for Personal Perspectives

Before sharing a fictional text with students, teachers will read the book and determine the author's purpose or theme. Next, they will create a list of value statements related to the theme. For example, if a book's theme involves friendship, the teacher might develop statements such as:

- "I try to be a good friend."
- "I like to make lots of friends."
- "Friends can be difficult sometimes."
- "It's important to have a lot of friends."
- "A good friend is someone who stands by your side."

Before introducing the book to the class, the teacher will instruct students to listen to a few statements and stand (or pop up) if they agree with them. After each statement, call on a few students—both sitting and standing—to describe why they agreed or disagreed with the statement. It is important to refrain from guiding them to one way of thinking; simply listen to their ideas and allow them to hear from their peers, too. Finally, introduce the book and tell the students that they will read to find out what the author wants us to know about friendship.

This I Believe

The teacher will distribute a piece of construction paper to each student and instruct them to think about a given topic (i.e., the theme of a book they are about to read). The teacher will ask an open-ended question and instruct the students to write an answer on their construction paper. For example, if the book is about a family tradition, the teacher might ask, "Name an important reason for spending time with your family." The students will hold up their answers on their construction paper and the teacher will arrange them in groups based on similar responses. If a few responses are more popular than others, the teacher might set a purpose such as, "Let's read to see if the author believes that one of our reasons is most important, too."

Cover Clues

Often, the illustrator will convey the story's theme or problem on the book cover so that the reader subconsciously considers the issues before even opening the book! The teacher should capitalize on this by holding up the book cover and posing the question, "What problem do you think the characters in the book will have to solve? How do you know?" Effective readers use visual information to make accurate predictions.

Then, the teacher will guide the students in *reading* the illustrations: consider the colors used, the thickness of the lines, the shapes (harsh geometric shapes that convey anxiety or trouble; or soft, organic shapes that convey calm and safety). Another clue lies in the font used for the book's title: are the letters fancy, thick, angular . . . ? Each font conveys a mood or plot line. As children and teacher discuss these visual elements, the teacher will list their ideas on the board and refer to them as the book is read aloud.

Why on Earth?

Before reading a book of fiction that conveys a social justice issue, significant historical event, or ethical dilemma, the teacher should ask the class a "Why" question that will pique their interest while drawing on their own lived experiences. For example, before reading a story about immigration, the teacher might ask, "Why do you think people would leave their country to live in the United States?" Students use their writing notebooks to compose a list of ideas, drawn from either their own experiences, or from stories told to them by family members, news media outlets, friends, etc. These latter sources provide "text-to-world connections" (Harvey & Goudvis, 2007, p. 100). The teacher should then have students volunteer to share their ideas, while writing them on the board.

As the story is read aloud, the teacher makes connections as appropriate from the list. After reading, the teacher takes a moment to have students add to their lists new ideas and insights they've gleaned from the story. The teacher adds their ideas to the class list and generates a discussion (and perhaps sets a purpose for action). The new ideas represent higher-level thinking because students synthesized their pre-reading ideas with the new insights in the story to create fresh ideas written in their own words.

Vocabulary Builder

Before reading a story about two characters facing a conflict, the teacher will select five interesting, content-based words from the book and list them on the board. Next, s/he will read them aloud, tracking his/her hand along each word and encouraging the class to join in to chorally read the words. The teacher will then show the book's cover and read the title aloud, and point out the two characters. The teacher will say, "All of these words are used by the author in this book."

The class will discuss the words, with the teacher guiding them toward defining unknown words. Finally, the teacher will refer to the cover of the book and ask the class to predict which words the author likely used with which character. The students will need to consider the illustrator's use of visual elements, facial expressions, etc. to assist them here. The teacher will list the words below each character's name as the students make their predictions. As the book is read aloud, students will listen for accuracy. After the book, they will reflect on the author's use of language to convey information about the characters.

CONCLUDING THOUGHTS

Effective readers are those who engage their minds in the text before they begin to read the words. Teachers need to model this process by intentionally inserting pre-reading activities into their read alouds. They need to read aloud excellent books during instruction of all content areas so that their beginning readers will understand that literacy is a skill that impacts their ability to learn new information, think about their world, appreciate artistic pursuits, and develop empathic understandings of people from all cultures. When teachers capitalize on moments available to them before engaging their students in reading a text, they convey the importance of setting a purpose for reading, anticipating content, synthesizing known information with new information, determining importance, and developing their academic vocabulary levels.

The literacy moments described in this chapter are meant to be brief activities that create opportunities for teachers to develop higher-level thinking skills. They engage readers in the active construction of meaning, which will enable them to comprehend the material in a way that allows them to take ownership of their learning processes. While some of these moments may take more time than others, their benefits show that it is time well spent. When teachers set aside a few minutes to access their students' schema and activate their minds for the upcoming text, they facilitate their students' abilities to see reading as more than a product—it is a process. Furthermore, they foster a love of reading and increase their beginning readers' comprehension skills along the way!

REFERENCES

Anderson, R. C. (1994). The role of the reader's schema in comprehension, learning, and memory (pp. 469–82). In R. B. Ruddell, M. R. Ruddell, and H. Singer (Eds.), *Theoretical models and processes of reading* (4th ed.). Newark, DE: International Reading Association.

Gallagher, K. (2004). *Deeper reading: Comprehending challenging texts, 4–12*. Portland, ME: Stenhouse.

Harvey, S., & Goudvis, A. (2007). *Strategies that work: Teaching comprehension for understanding and engagement* (2nd ed.). Portland, ME: Stenhouse.

Ostroff, W. L. (2016). *Cultivating curiosity in K–12 classrooms: How to promote and sustain deep learning*. Alexandria, VA: Association for Supervision and Curriculum Development (ASCD).

Rosenblatt, L. (1995). *Literature as exploration* (5th ed.). New York: Modern Language Association of America.

Chapter Eight

Literacy Moments That Foster Comprehension during Reading

The ebb and flow of an early-elementary classroom involves reading a variety of texts throughout all subject areas. When teachers intentionally integrate fiction and nonfiction literature across the curriculum, they create opportunities to teach not only the subject areas but also how to comprehend the information presented in those texts. Opportunities for literacy moments abound during content-area instruction while reading literature and other types of texts.

As teachers develop their knowledge of how to reinforce reading skills taught during language arts lessons, they will seek out moments during the reading of texts in all subjects to foster their students' application of those skills so that they become strategic readers (Routman, 1991). When teachers rely on commercial programs that emphasize teaching skills in isolation, students rarely transfer the skill strategically while reading authentic texts. Therefore, "a skill—no matter how well it has been taught—cannot be considered a strategy until the learner can use it purposefully and independently" (ibid., p. 134). The most effective way to ensure transference of comprehension strategies to authentic texts is to model this and guide beginning readers in the process while reading fiction and nonfiction literature throughout all subjects.

ASKING QUESTIONS TO ENGAGE STUDENTS IN CONSTRUCTING MEANING WHILE READING

When the class is reading a text, whether authentic literature, online article, song lyrics, poems, or content area textbook, the teacher must gauge the students' levels of comprehension. Doing so will serve several purposes: (1) the teacher will be able to assess the students' understanding of the information in the text; (2) the teacher will be able to model active thinking processes when reading the text; (3) the students will develop their comprehension skills as they read; (4) the students will be able to gauge their own levels of understanding as they read. Therefore, teachers need to shift their mindsets from asking questions at the end of the text (typically to test for understanding) and take time to ask questions while reading the text to serve the purpose of increasing their beginning readers' comprehension processes. After all, "generating questions while reading is perhaps the single strategy most prevalent in good readers and absent in poor ones" (Schwanenflugel & Knapp, 2016, p. 211).

In order to ensure that these questions are intentional and focused on constructive thinking and comprehension, teachers should use these literacy moments to develop their students' literal, inferential, and evaluative levels of thinking. These questions foster increasingly complex levels of inquiry. Following are descriptions of each type of question and the types of comprehension each level addresses.

Literal Questions

These fact-based questions encourage readers to focus on details by requiring them to locate information directly stated in the text. Often, these questions require readers to skim and scan the text to locate a fact explicitly stated by the author. Literal questions provide a type of scaffolding for beginning readers because they can help readers locate facts in a text in order to assist them in answering a higher-level question.

Teachers typically ask literal questions to nurture their readers' abilities in the following skills: recognizing the main idea, recalling facts, sequencing events, listing details, comparing and contrasting items, recognizing causes and effects. Here are a few sample questions for each of these comprehension elements.

Recognizing Main Idea

- Did the character learn something important? What does the book say about that?
- What happened when _____?
- What does the author say about _____?

Recalling Facts

- When did _____ happen? Who was involved? Where did they go?
- What are the characteristics of _____?
- Name three key facts we need to remember from this page.

Sequencing Events

- What happened first? Last?
- List the events that took place between ____ and ____.
- What has to happen before ____ can take place?

Listing Details

- As we read, let's fill in the information on this chart about each [animal, explorer, season, planet, etc.].
- List the words used to describe the main character as we read this page.
- How do you know that it is winter in this story so far? List the words used by the author as evidence.

Comparing and Contrasting Items

- What is the difference between ____ and ____?
- In what ways are the two main characters alike? How are they different?
- As we read, raise your hand when you notice the author giving us details about how the main character is changing.

Recognizing Causes and Effects

- Find the reason for ____ happening at this point in the story.
- As we read about plants, raise your hand when you notice a cause for what makes them grow.
- How did ____ affect ____?

Inferential Questions

These questions require the reader to engage in a close reading of the text. This is a very important skill because it demands the reader pay attention to information that is not explicitly conveyed in the body of the text. Instead, readers must read between the lines and deduce the author's implied meaning. This more complex level of thinking must be developed and nurtured through the careful construction of questions whose answers require the readers to synthesize two sources of information: literal details contained in the text and the readers' prior experiences or background knowledge about those details.

When teachers ask effective inferential questions, they must not only use them to give students practice with this type of thinking; they must also use them as opportunities to model *how* to answer them so that all students will develop this level of comprehension. For this reason, teachers should use a document camera to project the text on the whiteboard or smartboard so that s/he can model how to find literal information in the text, highlight it, and use it to "read between the lines" and answer the inferential question. Furthermore, when teachers follow the question up with "Why?" or "How do you know?" they essentially drive the readers back to the text for a close reading to locate literal information that will support their inferences.

Inferential questions provide practice in developing the following types of comprehension skills: making predictions, drawing conclusions, determining causes and/or effects, determining main idea, determining importance, and interpreting figurative language. Here are some potential questions that foster inferential thinking while reading a text.

Making Predictions

- Based on what we know about ____, what do you think will happen next?
- Do you believe ____ will ____? How do you know?
- Let's look at our list of characteristics we've made so far for the main character. Based on this information, what do you think s/he will do about ____?

Drawing Conclusions

- What is the author trying to tell us about ____? How do you know?
- Do you think the main character planned for ____ to happen? Why?
- Based on the facts listed here, what do you think caused ____ war?

Determining Causes and/or Effects

- Why do you suppose the main character did ____?
- What is the result of ____?
- If ____ happened, then what caused it?

Determining Main Idea and Theme

- At this point, why do you think the author wrote this story?
- What is the most important lesson we've learned so far?
- Based on what we know about ____, what is the author trying to tell us here?

Determining Importance

- Let's list the facts about ____ as we read this section. At the end of the section, we will decide which facts are important to remember as we move into the next section.
- Why did the author include this detail on this page? Is this significant?
- Which character trait is most important, given what we know about this character?

Interpreting Figurative Language

- What did the author mean by the phrase "_____"?
- Why did the author refer to the character as ____?
- Why would ____ be described as ____?

Evaluative Questions

These questions go beyond the lines of the text, requiring readers to think divergently about the content and engage in critical thinking. Here, readers must reflect on their prior experiences and background knowledge and use information as they read. They must synthesize these elements in order to formulate insights and participate in open-ended discussions prompted by such questions. The purpose of asking evaluative questions is to engage beginning readers in thinking and discussing ideas. These experientially based questions do not have any "correct" answers.

When teachers ask students evaluative questions while reading a text, they provide literacy moments that demand pausing for a quick, yet thought-provoking, small-group discussion. These are the quintessential think-pair-share discussions (Lyman, 1981) that emphasize active thinking and critical reasoning before moving on to the next section or page. Evaluative questions demand that the reader engage in the following types of critical thinking: making judgments, forming opinions, determining value or worth, determining fantasy versus reality, and determining validity. Ultimately, students who engage in thoughtful discussions will also hone their listening skills as they learn to value the opinions of others, even if they disagree.

Making Judgments

- Was it wrong for the main character to ____? Why do you think so?
- What would be the right thing to do in this situation?
- Who was right? Why?

Forming Opinions

- In your opinion, is it ethical for the character to ____?
- What would you do if . . . ?
- What do you think about ____?

Determining Value or Worth

- Was it worth it for this character in history to undergo _____ for ____ cause? Why do you think so?

- Would you have done ____ in this situation?
- Is this character's trait a good quality to have? Would s/he make a good friend?

Determining Fantasy versus Reality

- Could this really happen?
- Is this possible?
- In what way could this be true? False?

Determining Validity

- Is this information accurate based on your own experiences?
- Let's stop here and compare this information with the article we read yesterday. Do you think this new information is consistent with the ideas we read about this subject yesterday?
- Are these ideas still accepted in today's society? Why?

CLASSROOM ACTIVITIES THAT FOSTER ACTIVE THINKING DURING READING

Beginning readers thrive in print-rich classrooms. Word walls and charts not only reinforce content learned in class; they also provide a handy reference for young readers who need reminders related to decoding concepts, vocabulary terms, and written conventions. Why not use charts to assist these readers in their comprehension development, too? Since Durkin (1978) created the K-W-L chart, teachers have known that charts provide graphic organization tools for beginning readers that enhance their critical thinking and processing of both fiction and informational text.

Graphic Organizers

Through their use of graphic organizers, teachers can actively model thought processes and post information about how to comprehend text while the text is read by the children. As the text is read aloud, teachers will pause when they encounter a detail or inference or other comprehension element that they have decided to emphasize. Next, they will lead the students in filling out the chart, thinking aloud as they model the thought processes involved. Completed charts provide a reference for students during independent reading, as well as a structured way to organize their thoughts. Following are descriptions of charts that teachers can create with their students while reading a text to foster increased levels of comprehension.

Matrix of Details

When reading informational text that covers a lot of information and detail about key events, people, or scientific facts, teachers can help students keep track of details and engage them in active thinking by having the class fill in the information on a matrix as they read (see Table 8.1).

Table 8.1. Matrix of Information about Famous Inventors

Who?	When?	Where?	What?	Why?

Inferential Thinking Procedure

Teachers can provide a tangible way to make inferential thinking less abstract by demonstrating the process as a math problem. In this chart, teachers lay out how students can take literal information from the text and add it to what they already know about that information (their schema). The sum of these two parts equals their inference (see Table 8.2).

Table 8.2. Inferential Thinking Procedure

The text says: _____ +	I already know _____ =	Therefore, I infer _____ .

Question Webs (Harvey & Goudvis, 2007, p. 121)

Before reading an informational book about an issue, historical event, or scientific inquiry, teachers will first nurture their students' curiosity about the topic by asking them to generate a question that they want to think about before reading the book. The teacher will guide them toward an essential question that will be examined by the author of the book. Once the class has determined their main essential question, the teacher will write it on the board and draw a circle around it. As the book is read aloud, the teacher will pause and ask the students if any information has been provided on a given page that would help the class to answer their question. This is key in modeling for beginning readers how to determine importance: if the information does not pertain to the purpose or question that they are trying to answer, then it is not a significant point to focus on at this time (Fisher, Frey, and Lapp, 2009).

As students respond with information gleaned from the book, the teacher writes their ideas around the question to create a web of information. By the end of the book, the class will review the information around the question to develop their answers. They could write their ideas in their notebooks, discuss them with a small group, or work collaboratively to create a class response.

Read Like Writers

Teachers can draw students' attention to the expert writers in their classrooms: the authors of the books they read aloud and share with the class. If the class has been practicing the trait of word choice during their writing workshop, the teacher can set a purpose during a read aloud to be aware of the author's interesting word choice as they read. First, the teacher will model how to select an author's word choice that s/he finds meaningful for a personal reason. Once a word is noticed verbally, the teacher records it in the first column of a t-chart. After the teacher shares his/her reasons for selecting the word and talks about its definition, s/he writes the reason in the second column.

After initially modeling this process, the teacher should encourage students to pause while reading and share a word that they found to be powerful or thought-provoking. The teacher will then record the word and the reason on the chart and continue reading until another reader asks to pause for a word or phrase of interest. This process enables beginning readers to think about a writer's craft while focusing on a specific trait. It encourages them to consider using similar words or phrases in their own compositions. Teachers should have students create these t-charts in their writing notebooks so that they will be a handy reference for their own composition efforts. Finally, it creates a literacy moment rich in vocabulary development! See Table 8.3 for an example.

Table 8.3. Read Like Writers

Interesting words found in _____ [book title]	What makes them interesting to us:

Post-a-Thought

Before reading a picture book, the teacher will distribute a small stack of sticky notes to each student, or pair of students. Next, the teacher will set a purpose for reading the book, based on the main idea or information the author is conveying to the readers. Following this introduction, the teacher will place the book on a document camera and project it onto their smartboard. They will begin to read and then pause to examine the first illustration that contains key details or information related to the main idea. Here, the teacher will think aloud and talk about what s/he noticed that the illustrator included in the picture that will give a clue about the main idea/problem/theme/information of the book. The teacher will write the idea on his/her sticky note, and post it on the illustration.

As the picture and sticky note are projected on the smartboard, the teacher will take a screenshot and store it on the screen. Next, it's the students' turn to write key ideas conveyed in the illustrations and post them on the book. The teacher takes a screenshot, saves it, and continues reading. By the end of the book, the teacher will review each of the illustrations and the students' ideas posted around them. The class will use their ideas to construct a sentence stating the main idea, theme, or important information.

TEACHING BEGINNING READERS TO MONITOR THEIR COMPREHENSION

The process of reading for meaning is not a passive undertaking; readers must actively construct knowledge as they read. All readers need to have an inner dialogue with themselves as they read, constantly asking, "Does this make sense?" That is the key to monitoring their comprehension. However, while this is very important, it isn't enough to simply know when they are not able to fully understand the text. Readers need to know *what to do about it*. This is the difference between a competent reader and a struggling reader (Fisher, Frey, & Lapp, 2012).

Teachers of beginning readers need to intentionally create literacy moments that model, teach, and apply the process of self-monitoring while reading, as well as various fix-it strategies when readers become confused. Often, struggling readers will either give up or simply continue reading, hoping to figure it out along the way (Fisher, Frey, & Lapp, 2012). To avoid this response, teachers need to let their beginning readers in on the secrets of effective readers. The first step is to develop a list with the students of the habits of effective readers. This list will be a permanent part of the classroom's print environment (see Textbox 8.1)

> **TEXTBOX 8.1   SAMPLE CLASS LIST OF "FIX-IT" STRATEGIES**
>
> **What can we do when we don't understand what we're reading?**
> - Stop and reread
> - Slow down our reading pace
> - Reread the text aloud to hear yourself as you read
> - Ask questions about the text
> - Ask, "What do I know so far?"
> - Stop and try to form a picture in your mind of what you've just read about
> - Look at how the author structures the information in the text

Throughout the year, the teacher should intentionally pause during read alouds and check for comprehension, modeling and adding new fix-it strategies to the list. As each new strategy is added to the list, the teacher must model its use and teach it to the students before moving on in the read aloud. Its constant presence will serve as a reminder for students to think about a variety of options when comprehension breaks down. It will be a reference point for beginning readers during their independent reading time. Beginning readers will become empowered readers!

USING THINK ALOUDS DURING AUTHENTIC MOMENTS OF COMPREHENSION CONFUSION

What happens when a teacher is reading aloud to the class and s/he is experiencing a real moment of confusion? This is the best time to pause, tell the class that all readers have times when they don't understand the text, and think aloud as they reread the information slowly. During the think aloud, the teacher must intentionally model strategies that will remove the confusion and enhance comprehension.

For example, if the information needs to be clarified, teachers would pose questions to themselves about the information presented in the text. They would reread to find the answers, and think aloud as they make inferences that are elaborative in nature (i.e., they need more than one step in making connections between background knowledge and literal information). Perhaps the information contained should be visually represented in a diagram or chart—if so, then teachers would think about this in front of the students and draw the diagram on the board or in the margin of the text.

The significance of using think alouds while reading a text is that they provide students with a glimpse into the mind of the expert reader (the teacher) to see how that reader approaches a difficult text and fixes any confusion as they read. In such moments, teachers are conveying the importance of monitoring comprehension, thinking critically about text, and ultimately, how to strategically navigate their way back to full comprehension. These are very powerful literacy moments and need to be seized as learning opportunities.

CONCLUDING THOUGHTS

Teachers of beginning readers understand that their students need a lot of support as they learn to decode words, experience a variety of books, develop writing skills, and become motivated to read and learn. With all of this at play, it is important to also remember to pause and create or capitalize on literacy moments that will enhance comprehension while reading and enjoying a book, poem, article, song, etc. When teachers take the time to both demonstrate and directly instruct students on how to think critically as they read, they give their students access to society's literacy club (Smith, 1988). Each of the methods described in this chapter take only a few moments of time, but their rewards are limitless! As beginning readers develop their independence in decoding, they need to focus on strategies for constructing meaning and monitoring their thinking. These abilities will serve them well as they enter middle and upper elementary grades, where the emphasis will be on reading to learn new information.

REFERENCES

Fisher, D., Frey, N., and Lapp, D. (2009). *In a reading state of mind: Brain research, teacher modeling, and comprehension instruction.* Newark, DE: International Reading Association.

Fisher, D., Frey, N. and Lapp, D. (2012). *Teaching students to read like detectives: Comprehending, analyzing, and discussing text.* Bloomington, IN: Solution Tree Press.

Lyman, F. (1981). The responsive classroom discussion: The inclusion of all students. *Mainstreaming Digest.* University of Maryland, College Park, MD.

Routman, R. (1991). *Invitations: Changing as teachers and learners K–12.* Portsmouth, NH: Heinemann.

Schwanenflugel, P. J. and Knapp, N. F. (2016). *The psychology of reading: Theory and applications.* New York: Guilford Press.

Smith, F. (1988). *Joining the literacy club: Further essays into education.* Portsmouth, NH: Heinemann.

Chapter Nine

Post-Reading Activities

Why do we read a text? The answer to this question may depend upon the type of text we're reading. If we've read a work of fiction, we likely chose it for enjoyment, or to gain insight into an issue, topic, or person's lived experiences set in a fictionalized time or place. Perhaps we wanted to live vicariously through a character's journey of self-discovery. These are only a few reasons to read fiction. If we've read a work of nonfiction, we likely wanted to learn about a new topic, read more about a favorite subject, develop a new craft or skill, or gain insight into a real person's life story. Maybe we read a poem for the beauty of the rhythmic language used by the poet. Again, these are some, but certainly not all, of the reasons to read nonfiction texts.

One thing is certain: we did not read the text because we like to decode words. This is important for teachers of beginning readers to remember. Teachers may become focused on ensuring their budding readers blossom into fluency, causing them to overemphasize decoding skills over comprehension strategies when reading a text. As the content of Chapters 7 and 8 convey, the purpose of reading any text is to think, learn, grow, understand, analyze, and ultimately, possess new ways of being, knowing, and interacting with one another and our world.

The real question for early elementary teachers, therefore, is *How do we foster engagement with text and create a learning environment that allows it to impact the hearts and minds of our beginning readers?* The purpose of this chapter is to provide answers to this question through the implementation of literacy moments that occur immediately following the reading of a text. These are not meant to be elaborate activities—these are moments, a few minutes, meant to immerse our students in the ways that our literate community reacts to a work of literature that they've finished reading. In other words, there are no suggestions here that involve creating dioramas or mobiles. And, most importantly, there are no worksheets to download and print. Following are post-reading activities that allow time for beginning readers to think, react, and respond authentically to literature.

IMPROMPTU RESPONSES TO LITERATURE

A Moment of Silence

After reading a text that has been impactful for any number of reasons, teachers need to embrace a moment of silence. Here, everyone in the room sits quietly and just allows their minds to ruminate on their thoughts. Teachers may not always think about this as a post-reading activity because nothing tangible is happening: questions are not being asked and answered, pencils are not busily scratching out students' thoughts about the text, crayons aren't in hand, ready to draw pictures of favorite scenes. The class is simply thinking—including the teacher. This is key: the teacher remains in his/her spot in the classroom, visibly pondering the book along with the students. When the students start to move their bodies, shifting as if saying they're ready to move on, the teacher will ask them to share their thoughts and reactions. This is one of the most prevalent ways that society responds to literature, so teachers will serve their students well to carve out time for silence at the end of the book.

One Question

Why did the author write this book? By asking this one question, teachers allow time for their students to reflect and think about the author's purpose and the theme of the book or text. Through this question, beginning readers gain experience in thinking inferentially about the content in order to draw conclusions about purpose and theme. Furthermore, when teachers routinely ask this question, students will develop the habit of thinking about purpose and theme independently, paying careful attention to details and determining their importance as the book is read. They will anticipate their need to think about important content as they read.

One Word

Early in the school year, the teacher will scaffold students into this activity by modeling for them how to think about one word that would sum up a book or text the class just finished reading together. By the middle of the year, the teacher should be able to turn this around and structure a moment of silence by telling the class to think quietly about one word that they believe would sum up the book. Following their independent think time, have them turn to a friend or small group and each share their words. The group then determines the one word they felt was the most appropriate fit. Finally, the teacher will reach out to each group, listing their one word on the board. The class could vote on the one word from this list, or simply reflect on how each word is appropriate based on the reasoning given by each group.

So What?

Teachers can pose this question to the class upon the end of a read aloud. Students must turn and talk through their responses to this question, which requires them to think about the book's theme or author's purpose. After sufficient partnered discussion time, the teacher will regroup the whole class and have each pair share their answers. As the answers are revealed, the teacher will write them on the board, placing a check mark next to any duplicates. When all pairs have given their responses, the class will consider those with multiple check marks and discuss why they seem to be the more prevalent statements. The teacher will guide students through this discussion, using think alouds to scaffold their process in drawing conclusions and interpreting text.

Post a Thought

Teachers will encourage students to think about the text and form a personal response by distributing a 3 × 3 sticky note to each child before reading a text aloud. The teacher will prompt the students to listen and follow along, thinking about how this text makes them think about its topic, issue, or problem. After reading, the students will have time to write a sentence on their sticky note and post it on the board around the book (placed on the ledge), like thought bubbles. The teacher will read each note aloud, pausing for brief discussions as needed. To extend this activity, the teacher would rearrange the notes, grouping them by similarity, to create a spontaneous bar graph. Here, the teacher could facilitate quantitative reasoning about the number of more prevalent responses, etc.

SMALL-GROUP DISCUSSIONS

The intentional use of small-group discussions is very important to the development of beginning readers because these discussions ensure that all voices in the room are heard. Many students may be intimidated by the thought of volunteering to answer a question in front of the whole class. Typically, the more vocal students will raise their hands the most often, causing the same voices to be heard over those of their peers. In small-group discussions, however, all students will have more opportunities to enter into a conversation with their peers.

Furthermore, when teachers engage students in authentic, relevant forms of discussion and communication, they foster a culturally responsive learning environment that encourages students to actively construct their knowledge, critically analyze content and apply it to the real world (Gay, 2000). Many of the activities presented in this book revolve around small-group discussions. Here are a few additional post-reading discussion activities.

Question Pass

This idea is based on Daniels' and Zemelman's "written conversation" activity (2004, p. 159). After reading a text, the teacher distributes a sheet of paper to each student and puts them into small groups of three to four students. The students begin by independently writing at the top of the paper a question about the book that comes to mind. Next, the students pass their question to the left and read their peer's question silently. The students have a few minutes to quickly write a response to the question. When the teacher says, "pass," all students finish their thoughts and pass the paper to the left.

The teacher instructs the students to read the question and the first answer. They then write their own response below the first answer and pass it when time is up. An important rule here is "no dittos." In other words, each student must think about an original response to write. This continues until the students end up with their original question. The teacher gives them time to silently read their peers' written responses. Finally, time is given for the groups to discuss their questions and answers. The teacher concludes the activity by having each group report out, describing some of the questions and generally summing up their discussions.

Curiosities and Wonderings

During the reading of a text, the teacher will engage the students in keeping a list of new information learned from the author. The teacher could encourage all students to participate by having them put their thumb up whenever they encounter a new concept or a point of clarification. The teacher will call on these students to share their ideas and write them on the board. After reading, small groups of students will discuss the new information, commenting on their own "aha" moments, too.

Next, the teacher will challenge the groups to discuss questions they now have based on new curiosities. Teachers could prompt their thinking by having each group complete the statement: "We wonder why . . ." or "We are curious about . . ." Each group will have a sentence strip upon which to write out their questions or sentences and post them on the board to discuss as a whole class.

Author's Intention and Author's Impact

When authors compose a text, they are sending a message to their readers. Each reader has his/her own identity and lived experiences. Their identities will influence how they interpret the author's message. When teachers make time after reading a book to investigate how readers may interpret the message, they create moments that allow beginning readers to explore topics such as: implicit bias, cultural diversity, social justice, etc.

While reading a text, the teacher will set a purpose for students' thinking about impact by having them create a t-chart in their writing notebooks. On the left side, students will write "Author's Message" and they will label the right column "My Thoughts About It" (based on Ahmed, 2018, p. 118). As the text is read, the teacher will pause for students to jot down information or ideas in which they believe the author intended to convey a message.

After reading, students will have time to fill in the right column independently, noting their thoughts about each message. Finally, small groups will gather to share their charts and discuss any differences in interpretations of the author's messages. This is most beneficial as a small-group activity after the teacher has modeled it during a whole-class activity early in the school year.

WRITTEN RESPONSES

While small-group and whole-class discussions are very important to beginning readers' development of comprehension processes, "words die in the air," as one very influential professor once stated. Writing offers students the opportunity to make their thoughts permanent. It also encourages the composition of new knowledge and insights. Finally, the act of writing fosters beginning readers' ability to make abstract thoughts more concrete. When written responses are integrated into literacy moments, teachers enable beginning readers to understand the reading-writing connection.

Write from a List (Buckner, 2005)

This activity promotes thinking creatively and metacognitively about a text. Here, the teacher has students think about a specific key idea or concept conveyed by the author. The students must then write a list of ideas in their writing notebooks. This is a form of independent brainstorming, in which the most obvious ideas typically come first and then the more interesting, creative ideas follow. To ensure creative thinking, the teacher should require a set amount of ideas put on their lists ("Make a list of ten ideas . . ."). This will require the students to think beyond the obvious.

Once the lists are completed—or near completion—the students must re-read their list and put an asterisk next to their top three favorite ideas. This portion of the activity nurtures their metacognition as they have to think about their own thinking and evaluate their own ideas. Finally, the students must pick their favorite of the top three and rewrite it at the top of the next page in their notebook. It will serve as a topic sentence for a paragraph they will write that elaborates on their favorite idea.

Found Poems

This activity is most effective as an extension of the "Read Like Writers" activity described in Chapter 8. While reading, the teacher will encourage students to notice the author's use of interesting phrases or statements. The teacher will write them down as they are shared aloud during the reading.

As a post-reading response, the teacher will have the students independently select various phrases, words, and statements from the list and arrange them into poetic form. In other words, the students are using the found phrases and making them their own by rearranging them to reflect their personal responses to the text. This literacy moment could evolve into a published work by having the students copy their final version of their poems onto 12 × 18 construction paper and illustrating them for display in the room.

Poetic Responses

Beginning readers will develop confidence in writing using a poetic framework that scaffolds their process in composing written responses. Here are a couple of examples.

List Poems

After reading a book about any topic or theme, teachers should instruct students to think about the topic and how they would define or describe it.

Next, they write a sentence fragment on the board and have students generate ideas to complete the sentence based on their reflections from the book. For example, after reading *The Snowy Day* (Keats, 1962), the teacher would write "Snow is _____." The teacher then leads the class in developing ideas, ranging from one-word answers ("Snow is awesome." "Snow is cold.") to similes or metaphors ("Snow is like a blanket for tulips waiting to grow in the spring.") Finally, the teacher will challenge students to compose their own list poem of three to five lines in their notebooks, each line starting with "Snow is ____."

Acrostics

After reading a picture book about an issue or with a compelling theme, the teacher would write the one-word issue or theme vertically and have them copy it into their notebooks. Next, the teacher will model how to think about a word or phrase that begins with the first letter in the word and relates to the issue, characters, theme, etc. After modeling the first several letters, have the students complete the acrostic in their notebooks.

Concrete Poems

As a text is read together with the class, the teacher instructs the students to raise their hands when they encounter an interesting word. The teacher will list each word on the board as the students name them. After reading, the teacher will lead the class in chorally reading the list of words. If words need to be discussed and defined, the teacher will lead the class in this process. Next, the teacher will ask students to think about a shape that would be a good representative of the theme or concept from the text.

Students will write the title of the book on a new page in their notebook and then lightly draw the outline of the shape. Finally, the teacher will instruct the students to use the words from the list, and any additional words they think of that pertain to the theme or concept of the book, and arrange them creatively around the perimeter of the shape. When they've finished, they will each have a personalized concrete poem to share with the class.

Reporter Questions

When children have finished a book, the teacher should lead them in a discussion about the main character's development: his/her initial actions, the problem s/he had to solve, his/her decisions made and ways s/he solved the problem, etc. Next, the teacher has the students imagine they are reporters that want to write an article about this character and how s/he solved her/his problem. Have students write in their notebook a series of questions they'd like to ask the character. If time permits, the students could each take turns asking a partner their questions and having the partner answer in character. When students have to think of questions, rather than answer teachers' questions, they learn to think more critically about the text.

Word Collage

During the reading of a text, the teacher will engage the students in noticing unique academic language used by the author (especially for informational books), as well as colorful adjectives, verbs, nouns, adverbs, etc. The teacher will read aloud, pause for students to independently record their word choices from that page, and continue on in this format until the end of the book. After reading, the teacher will distribute a sheet of 9 × 12 construction paper and instruct the students to arrange their words creatively, using a variety of crayon colors, and making important words in larger fonts than other words. Students should have the opportunity to share their word collages with the class to discuss their word choices and their thoughts on how they arranged them.

CONCLUDING THOUGHTS

When teachers intentionally create literacy moments after reading any type of text, they communicate to their students that readers transact with the text to create meaning (Rosenblatt, 1995). The ultimate purpose for reading any text is to think about the content the author is conveying through the printed word and the illustrator conveys through visual elements. The type of thinking required involves more than regurgitating answers to questions designed to test the reader.

Instead, teachers must set aside time to interact with their students meaningfully about the issues, themes, concepts, information, celebrations, entertainments, etc. contained in the texts they've read together. The post-reading literacy moments described in this chapter are meant to inspire teachers of beginning readers to seek new and innovative ways to engage their students in critical thinking and reflecting about text.

REFERENCES

Ahmed, S. (2018). *Being the change: Lessons and strategies to teach social comprehension.* Portsmouth, NH: Heinemann.

Buckner, A. (2005). *Notebook know-how: Strategies for the writer's notebook.* Portland, ME: Stenhouse.

Daniels, H., & Zemelman, S. (2004). *Subjects matter: Exceeding standards through powerful content-area reading.* Portsmouth, NH: Heinemann.

Gay, G. (2000). *Culturally responsive teaching: Theory, research & practice.* New York: Teachers College Press.

Rosenblatt, L. (1995). *Literature as exploration* (5th ed.). New York: Modern Language Association of America.

CHILDREN'S BOOKS CITED

Keats, E. (1962). *The snowy day.* New York: Viking Books for Young Readers.

Appendix

*Diverse Children's Authors
and Their Birthdays*

Month	Author's Name	Birthdate	Genre	Titles
September	Margarita Engle	Sept. 2	picture books; biographies	All the Way to Havana; Bravo!; The Flying Girl: How Aida de Acosta Learned to Soar
	Gloria Jean Pinkney	Sept. 5	picture books	Back Home; The Sunday Outing; Music From Our Lord's Holy Heaven: African-American Spirituals
	Andrea Davis Pinkney	Sept. 25	picture books	A Poem for Peter; Martin and Mahalia: His Words, Her Songs; Sit-In: How Four Friends Stood Up by Sitting Down; Sojourner Truth's Step-Stomp Stride
	Janet Wong	Sept. 30	picture books; poetry	Apple Pie Fourth of July; Minn and Jake; Knock on Wood: Poems about Superstitions; This Next New Year; The Poetry Friday Anthology for Celebrations (with Sylvia Vardell); Good Luck Gold
October	Faith Ringgold	Oct. 8	picture books	Tar Beach; Aunt Harriet's Underground Railroad in the Sky; Harlem Renaissance Party; Bronzeville Boys and Girls; We Came to America
	Elisa Kleven	Oct. 14	picture books	Abuela (illustrator); Isla (illustrator); Hooray, a Piñata!; Ernst; The Carousel
	Christopher Myers, illustrator	Oct. 17	picture books	H.O.R.S.E.: A Game of Basketball and Imagination; Harlem; Jazz; Black Cat; Jabberwocky
	Monica Brown	Oct. 24	picture books; biographies	Chavela and the Magic Bubble; My Name is Celia: The Life of Celia Cruz; Tito Puente: Mambo King
November	Pat Cummings	Nov. 9	picture books	Clean Your Room, Harvey Moon; My Aunt Came Back; Ananse and the Lizard: A West African Tale; Angel Baby; Harvey Moon, Museum Boy
	Carmen T. Bernier-Grand	Nov. 22	picture book biographies; early readers	Diego: Bigger than Life; Frida: ¡Viva la Viva! Long Live Life!; César: ¡Sí, Se Puede! Yes, We Can!; Juan Bobo: Four Folktales from Puerto Rico

	Ed Young	Nov. 28	picture books	Lon Po Po: A Red Riding Hood Story from China; Seven Blind Mice; The House Baba Built: An Artist's Childhood in China
December	George Ancona	Dec. 4	Informational photo essays	El Piñatero/The Piñata Maker; Barrio: José's Neighborhood; Mi Barrio: My Neighborhood
	Raul Colón	Dec. 17	picture books	Doña Flor: A Tall Tale About a Giant Woman with a Great Big Heart; Draw!; A Weave of Words (illustrator)
	Pam Muñoz Ryan	Dec. 25	picture books; middle-grade novels	Tony Baloney; Rice and Beans; Amelia and Eleanor Go for a Ride; Tony Baloney: Pen Pal (early reader); Riding Freedom
January	Floyd Cooper	Jan. 8	picture books	Jump!: From the Life of Michael Jordan; The Ring Bearer; Max and the Tag-Along Moon; Willie and the All-Stars
	Vera B. Williams	Jan. 28	picture books	A Chair for My Mother, Something Special for Me; Music, Music for Everyone; A Chair for Always
	Bryan Collier, illustrator	Jan. 31	picture books; biographies	Martin's Big Words; Rosa; Dave the Potter; Uptown
February	Matt de la Peña	Feb. 9	picture books; biographies; YA books	A Nation of Hope: The Story of Boxing Legend Joe Louis; Last Stop on Market Street
	Jacqueline Woodson	Feb. 12	picture books; middle-grade novels; YA novels	Show Way; Each Kindness; The Day You Begin; The Other Side; This Is the Rope: A Story from the Great Migration; Coming on Home Soon
	Carol Boston Weatherford	Feb. 13	picture books; biographies	Freedom in Congo Square; Juneteenth Jamboree; Voice for Freedom: Fannie Lou Hammer; Moses: When Harriet Tubman Led Her People to Freedom
	Barbara Joosse	Feb. 18	picture books	Mama, Do You Love Me?; Grandma Calls Me Beautiful; Sleepover at Gramma's House

(Continued)

(Continued)

Month	Author's Name	Birthdate	Genre	Titles
March	Chris Raschka	Mar. 6	picture books	Yo! Yes?; The Purple Balloon; Waffle; The Hello Goodbye Window
	Debbie Ridpath Ohi	Mar. 29	picture books	Max & Eva; Where Are My Books?; I'm series (illustrator)
April	Jerdine Nolen	Apr. 6	picture books; middle-grade novels	Big Jabe; In My Momma's Kitchen; Irene's Wish; Thunder Rose; Bradford Street Buddies (early reader series)
	Gary Soto	Apr. 12	picture books; poetry; middle-grade novels	If the Shoe Fits; Too Many Tamales; Lucky Luis; Chato's Kitchen; Chato and the Party Animals; Big Bushy Mustache; Snapshots from the Wedding
	Javaka Steptoe, illustrator	Apr. 19	picture books	Hot Day on Abbott Avenue; Amiri & Odette: A Love Story; What's Special about Me?; Rain Play
May	Kadir Nelson, illustrator	May 15	picture books	Big Jabe; Nelson Mandela; Henry's Freedom Box; Hewitt Anderson's Great Big Life; Ellington Was Not a Street; Dancing in the Wings
	Grace Lin	May 17	picture books	Dim Sum for Everyone; Ling and Ting: Not Exactly the Same (early reader); Kite Flying; The Ugly Vegetables
	Arthur Dorros	May 19	picture books; informational books	Abuela; Abuelo; Isla; Mamá and Me; Papá and Me; Julio's Magic; Feel the Wind; This Is My House

Reference List

Ahmed, S. (2018). *Being the change: Lessons and strategies to teach social comprehension*. Portsmouth, NH: Heinemann.

Allen, J. (1999). *Words, words, words: Teaching vocabulary in grades 4–12*. York, ME: Stenhouse.

Anderson, R. C. (1994). The role of the reader's schema in comprehension, learning, and memory (pp. 469–82). In R. B. Ruddell, M. R. Ruddell, and H. Singer (Eds.), *Theoretical models and processes of reading* (4th ed.). Newark, DE: International Reading Association.

Applegate, A., & Applegate, M. D. (2004). The Peter effect: Reading habits and attitudes of preservice teachers. *The Reading Teacher, 57*, pp. 554–63.

Bartolomé, L. (1994). Beyond the methods fetish: Toward a humanizing pedagogy. *Harvard Review, 64*, 173–94.

Buckner, A. (2005). *Notebook know-how: Strategies for the writer's notebook*. Portland, ME: Stenhouse.

Cameron, J. (1992). *The artist's way: A spiritual path to higher creativity*. New York: Penguin Putnam, Inc.

Clemens, S. G. (2009). Art in the classroom: Making every day special. Retrieved from http://webshare.northseattle.edu/fam180/topics/art/Art%20in%20the%20 Classroom.htm

Compton-Lilly, C. (2003). *Reading families: The literate lives of urban children*. New York: Teachers College Press.

Cornett, C. (2015). *Creating meaning through literature and the arts: Arts integration for classroom teachers* (5th ed.). Boston, MA: Pearson.

Cowhey, M. (2006). *Black ants and Buddhists: Thinking critically and teaching differently in the primary grades*. Portland, ME: Stenhouse Publishers.

Cunningham, P., Hall, D. P., & Cunningham, J. W. (2000). *Guided reading the four-blocks way*. Greensboro, NC: Carson-Dellosa Publishing.

Daniels, H., & Zemelman, S. (2004). *Subjects matter: Exceeding standards through powerful content-area reading*. Portsmouth, NH: Heinemann.

Eisner, E. (1983). *Beyond creating*. Los Angeles: Getty Center for Education in Art.

Fisher, D., Frey, N., & Lapp, D. (2009). *In a reading state of mind: Brain research, teacher modeling, and comprehension instruction*. Newark, DE: International Reading Association.

Fisher, D., Frey, N., & Lapp, D. (2012). *Teaching students to read like detectives: Comprehending, analyzing, and discussing text*. Bloomington, IN: Solution Tree Press.

Fleming, J., Catapano, S., Thompson, C. M., & Ruvalcaba Carrillo, S. (2016). *More mirrors in the classroom: Using urban children's literature to increase literacy*. Lanham, MD: Rowman & Littlefield.

Flynn, E. (2016). Language-rich early childhood classroom: Simple but powerful beginnings. *The Reading Teacher, 70*, 159–66.

Gallagher, K. (2003). *Reading reasons: Motivational mini lessons for middle and high school*. Portland, ME: Stenhouse.

Gallagher, K. (2004). *Deeper reading: Comprehending challenging texts, 4–12*. Portland, ME: Stenhouse.

Gay, G. (2000). *Culturally responsive teaching: Theory, research, & practice*. New York: Teachers College Press.

Graves, D. (1994). *A fresh look at writing*. Portsmouth, NH: Heinemann.

Harvey, S., & Goudvis, A. (2007). *Strategies that work: Teaching comprehension for understanding and engagement* (2nd ed.). Portland, ME: Stenhouse.

Hoffman, J. (2011). Coconstructing meaning: Interactive literary discussions in Kindergarten read alouds. *The Reading Teacher, 65*, 183–94.

Hollie, S. (2012). *Culturally and linguistically responsive teaching and learning: Classroom practices for student success*. Huntington Beach, CA: Shell Education.

International Reading Association. (2000). *Providing books and other print materials for classroom and school libraries: A position statement of the International Reading Association*. Newark, DE: International Reading Association.

Justice, L. M., Kaderavek, J. M., Fan, X., Sofka, A., & Hunt, A. (2009). Accelerating preschoolers' early literacy development through classroom-based teacher-child storybook reading and explicit print referencing. *Language, Speech, and Hearing Services in Schools, 40*, 67–85.

Kiefer, B. (1995). *The potential of picture books: From visual literacy to aesthetic understanding*. Englewood Cliffs, NJ: Prentice Hall.

Labbo, L. D. (2005). From morning message to digital morning message: Moving from the tried and true to the new. *The Reading Teacher, 58*, 782–85.

Ladson-Billings, G. (1995). But that's just good teaching! The case for culturally relevant pedagogy. *Theory into Practice, 34*(3), 159–65.

Ladson-Billings, G. (1992). Culturally relevant teaching: The key to making multicultural education work. In C. A. Grant (Ed.), *Research and multicultural education* (pp. 106–21). London: Falmer Press.

Lyman, F. (1981). The responsive classroom discussion: The inclusion of all students. *Mainstreaming Digest*. University of Maryland, College Park, MD.

National Endowment for the Arts. (2006). *The arts and civic engagement: Involved in arts, involved in life*. Washington, DC: National Endowment for the Arts.

Ostroff, W. L. (2016). *Cultivating curiosity in K–12 classrooms: How to promote and sustain deep learning.* Alexandria, VA: Association for Supervision and Curriculum Development (ASCD).

Pressley, M. (2000). What should comprehension instruction be the instruction of? (pp. 545–61). In M. Kamil, P. Mosenthal, P. D. Pearson, & R. Barr (Eds.), *Handbook of reading research: Volume III.* Mahwah, NJ: Lawrence Erlbaum Associates.

Rosenblatt, L. (1995). *Literature as exploration* (5th ed.). New York: Modern Language Association of America.

Routman, R. (1991). *Invitations: Changing as teachers and learners K–12.* Portsmouth, NH: Heinemann.

Ruddell, R. (2005). *Teaching children to read and write: Becoming an effective literacy teacher* (4th ed.). Boston, MA: Allyn & Bacon.

Rumelhart, D. E. (1994). Toward an interactive model of reading. In R. B. Ruddell, M. R. Ruddell, & H. Singer (Eds.), *Theoretical models and processes of reading* (4th ed.) (pp. 864–94). Newark, DE: International Reading Association.

Schwanenflugel, P. J., & Knapp, N. F. (2016). *The psychology of reading: Theory and applications.* New York: Guilford Press.

Smith, F. (1988). *Joining the literacy club: Further essays into education.* Portsmouth, NH: Heinemann.

Staib, M. (1928). A classroom library. *The English Journal, 17*(9), 762–65.

Stanovich, K. (1986). Matthew effects in reading: Some consequences of individual differences in the acquisition of literacy. *Reading Research Quarterly, 22,* 360–407.

Stauffer, R. G. (1970). *The language-experience approach to the teaching of reading.* New York: Harper & Row.

Wasik, B. A. & Hindman, A. H. (2011). The morning message in early childhood classrooms: Guidelines for best practices. *Early Childhood Education, 39,* 183–89.

Witter-Easley, J. (2015). Bringing books to life: Revitalize your classroom library with interactive book displays. *Literacy Today,* July/August, 24–5.

Witter-Easley, J. (2012). *Happy birthday, dear author!* Madison, WI: Upstart Books.

Children's Books Cited

Ackerman, K. (1988). *Song and dance man.* New York: Scholastic.
Adoff, A. (2000). *Touch the poem.* New York: Blue Sky Press.
Blos, J. (1994). *In the days before now: An autobiographical note by Margaret Wise Brown.* New York: Simon & Schuster.
Bridges, R. (1999). *Through my eyes.* New York: Scholastic.
Briggs, R. (1978). *The snowman.* New York: Random House.
Bryan, A. (2009). *Ashley Bryan: Words to my life's song.* New York: Atheneum.
Carle, E. (2011). *The artist who painted a blue horse.* New York: Philomel.
Cole, J. (1989). *Anna Banana: 101 jump-rope rhymes.* New York: William Morrow & Co.
Cole, J. & Calmenson, S. (1993). *Six sick sheep: 1010 tongue twisters.* New York: William Morrow & Co.
Cooney, B. (1982). *Miss Rumphius.* New York: Trumpet.
Crews, D. (1991). *Bigmama's.* New York: Trumpet.
Croza, L. (2010). *I know here.* Toronto: Groundwood Books.
dePaola, T. (1989). *The art lesson.* New York: G. P. Putnam's Sons.
dePaola, T. (1993). *Tom.* New York: Scholastic.
deRegniers, B. S., Moore, E., White, M. M., & Carr, J. (Eds.). (1988). *Sing a song of popcorn: Every child's book of poems.* New York: Scholastic.
Diller, J. (2013). *Mystery of the ballerina ghost: Austria (Pack-n-Go Girls Adventures Vol. 1).* Colorado Springs, CO: WorldTrek Publishing.
Dotlitch, R. K. (2004). *Over in the pink house: New jump rope rhymes.* Honesdale, PA: Boyds Mills Press.
Draper, S. (2011). *The buried bones: Clubhouse Mysteries.* New York: Aladdin.
Fanelli, S. (1995). *My map book.* New York: HarperCollins.
Flournoy, V. (1985). *The patchwork quilt.* New York: Dial.
Fox, M. (1989). *Wilfrid Gordon McDonald Partridge.* La Jolla, CA: Kane/Miller Books.
Gibson, R. (1995). *What shall I draw?* London: Usborne Books.

Gibson, R. (1997). *I can crayon*. London: Usborne Books.
Gibson, R. (1998). *I can draw animals*. London: Usborne Books.
Gibson, R. (2000). *I can draw people*. London: Usborne Books.
Giovanni, N. (Ed.) (2008). *Hip-hop speaks to children: A celebration of poetry with a beat*. Naperville, IL: Sourcebooks, Inc.
Greenfield, E. (1991). *Night on Neighborhood Street*. New York: Picture Puffins/Penguin Books.
Grimes, N. (2001). *A pocketful of poems*. New York: Clarion Books.
Hague, M. (1993). *Teddy bear, teddy bear: A classic action rhyme*. New York: William Morrow & Co.
Hathorn, L. (1994). *Way home*. New York: Crown.
Hoberman, M. (1991). *Fathers, mothers, sisters, brothers: A collection of family poems*. New York: Puffin/Penguin Books.
Hoberman, M. (2001). *You read to me, I'll read to you: Very short stories to read together*. Boston, MA: Little, Brown.
Hoffman, M. (2002). *The colour of home*. New York: Penguin Putnam Books.
Houston, G. (1992). *My Great Aunt Arizona*. New York: HarperCollins.
Howard, E. F. (1991). *Aunt Flossie's hats (and crab cakes later)*. Boston: Clarion Books.
Janeczko, P. (2001). *A poke in the I: A collection of concrete poems*. Somerville, MA: Candlewick Press.
Janeczko, P. (2005). *A kick in the head: An everyday guide to poetic forms*. Somerville, MA: Candlewick Press.
Keats, E. (1962). *The snowy day*. New York: Viking Books for Young Readers.
Khan, R. (2010). *Big red lollipop*. New York: Viking.
King, Jr., M. L. (2012). *I have a dream: Book & CD*. (Illustrated by Kadir Nelson). New York: Random House.
Kurtz, J. (2005). *In the small, small night*. New York: Greenwillow Books.
Kuskin, K. (2003). *Moon, have you met my mother?* New York: HarperCollins.
Laínez, R. C., & Accardo, A. (2004). *Waiting for Papá/Esperando a Papá*. Houston, TX: Piñata Books.
Lewis, J. P. (1990). *A hippopotamusn't*. New York: Trumpet Books.
Martin Jr., B., & Archambault, J. (1987). *Knots on a counting rope*. New York: Trumpet.
Marzollo, J. (1991). *I spy: A book of picture riddles*. New York: Scholastic.
McCall Smith, A. (2012). *The great cake mystery: Precious Ramotswe's very first case*. New York: Anchor Books.
Micklethwait, L. (1992). *I spy: An alphabet in art*. New York: HarperCollins.
Micklethwait, L. (1993). *A child's book of art: Great pictures—first words*. New York: DK Publishing.
Micklethwait, L. (1996). *A child's book of play in art*. New York: DK Publishing.
Micklethwait, L. (2004). *I spy shapes in art*. New York: Greenwillow Books.
Micklethwait, L. (2007). *I spy colors in art*. New York: Greenwillow Books.
Micklethwait, L. (2008). *Children: A first art book*. London: Frances Lincoln Children's Books.

Milne, A. A. (1992). *Now we are six!* New York: Puffin Books.
O'Donnell, L. (2015). *The case of the snack snatcher: West Meadows detectives.* Toronto: OwlKids Books.
O'Neill, M. (1961). *Hailstones and halibut bones: Adventures in color.* New York: Doubleday & Doubleday, Inc.
Opie, I., & Opie, P. (1992). *I saw Esau: The schoolchild's pocket book.* Cambridge, MA: Candlewick Press.
Park, F. (2002). *Good-bye, 382 Shin Dang Dong.* Des Moines, IA: National Geographic Children's Books.
Perkins, L. R. (2007). *Pictures from our vacation.* New York: Greenwillow Books.
Prelutsky, J. (1977). *It's Halloween.* New York: Scholastic.
Prelutsky, J. (1983). *It's Valentine's Day.* New York: Scholastic.
Prelutsky, J. (Ed.). (1983). *The Random House book of poetry.* New York: Random House.
Prelutsky, J. (1984). *The new kid on the block.* New York: Greenwillow.
Prelutsky, J. (1986). *Ride a purple pelican.* New York: Greenwillow.
Prelutsky, J. (1989). *Poems of A. Nonny Mouse.* New York: Alfred A. Knopf.
Polacco, P. (1991). *The keeping quilt.* New York: Simon & Schuster.
Raczka, B. (2003). *Art is.* Minneapolis, MN: Millbrook Press.
Raczka, B. (2003). *More than meets the eye: Seeing art with all five senses.* Minneapolis, MN: Millbrook Press.
Raczka, B. (2006). *3-D ABC: A sculptural alphabet.* Minneapolis, MN: Millbrook Press.
Raczka, B. (2009). *Artful reading.* Minneapolis, MN: Millbrook Press.
Raczka, B. (2009). *Name that style: all about isms in art.* Minneapolis, MN: Millbrook Press.
Raczka, B. (2009). *No one saw: Ordinary things through the eyes of an artist.* Minneapolis, MN: Millbrook Press.
Raczka, B. (2009). *Speaking of art: Colorful quotes by famous painters.* Minneapolis, MN: Millbrook Press.
Raczka, B. (2016). *Wet cement: A mix of concrete poems.* New York: Roaring Brook Press.
Roemer, H. (2004). *Come to my party: And other shape poems.* New York: Henry Holt.
Rylant, C. (1982). *When I was young in the mountains.* New York: E. P. Dutton.
Sanna, F. (2016). *The journey.* London: Flying Eye Books.
Say, A. (1993). *Grandfather's journey.* New York: Houghton Mifflin.
Sharmat, M. W. (1972). *Nate the great.* Scholastic: New York.
Sendak, M. (1962). *Chicken soup with rice: A book of months.* New York: Scholastic.
Shelby, A. (1995). *Homeplace.* London: Orchard Books.
Silverstein, S. (1974). *Where the sidewalk ends.* New York: Harper & Row.
Silverstein, S. (1981). *A light in the attic.* New York: Harper & Row.
Stevenson, J. (1994). *Fun, no fun.* New York: Greenwillow Books.
Stevenson, R. L. (1966). *A child's garden of verses.* Oxford: Oxford University Press.
The Real Mother Goose. (1944). New York: Checkerboard Press.

Williams, D. (1993). *Grandma Essie's covered wagon*. New York: Alfred A. Knopf.
Williams, V. (1982). *A chair for my mother*. New York: Scholastic.
Wong, J. (2002). *Apple pie 4th of July*. Orlando, FL: Harcourt.
Wyeth, S. D. (2013). *The granddaughter necklace*. New York: Arthur A. Levine Books.
Yolen, J. (1991). *All those secrets of the world*. Boston: Little, Brown.
Yolen, J. (1987). *Owl moon*. New York: Scholastic.
Young, E. (2011). *The house Baba built: An artist's childhood in China*. Boston, MA: Little, Brown.

About the Author

Jacqueline Witter-Easley, EdD, is dean of the Division of Professional Studies at Carthage College in Kenosha, Wisconsin, where she also serves as professor in the Education Department. At Carthage, she teaches courses in the methods of teaching reading and language arts in both elementary and secondary classrooms, as well as courses in children's literature and creative arts instruction. She recently co-created the college's new minor in Urban Education. Dr. Easley is a former elementary teacher, primarily in grades one and two. She was also an assistant children's librarian in her local public library where she created a variety of children's programs for the community. Her research interests include integrating children's literature across the curriculum, culturally responsive literacy instruction, and visual literacy.

www.ingramcontent.com/pod-product-compliance
Lightning Source LLC
Chambersburg PA
CBHW022015300426
44117CB00005B/206